# HOMES
## & GARDENS

# *Transforming*
# THE INTERIOR

# *Transforming*
# THE INTERIOR

JUDITH WILSON

conran
OCTOPUS

First published in 1998 by
Conran Octopus Limited
2-4 Heron Quays
London E14 4JP
Reprinted in 2000

Homes & Gardens is published
in the UK by IPC Magazines Ltd
Kings Reach Tower, Stamford Street,
London SE1 9LS

**Commissioning Editor:** Denny Hemming
**Managing Editor:** Catriona Woodburn
**Editorial Assistant:** Paula Hardy
**Art Editor:** Alison Fenton
**Picture Researcher:** Rachel Davies
**Production Controller:** Julian Deeming

British Library
Cataloguing-in-Publication Data
A catalogue record for this book is
available from the British Library
ISBN 1 85029 997 8

Printed in China

# Contents

# Introduction

*Decorating is an emotive issue. Just the thought of it inspires dreams and plans, private passions, the chance to realize new moods, trends and a fresh way of living. There are luscious colours to try, patterns to explore, shapes, spaces and light with which to experiment. Nearly all of us embrace the chance to redecorate with enthusiasm and a positive spirit. But the road to redecoration is never an easy one, and even the most strong-minded designer can suffer moments of self-doubt.*

**Above and Opposite** Fresh perspectives. Inspiration for a vibrant decorating scheme comes as readily from a fleeting image as from a supplier's colour swatch. The fiery red and intense yellow ochre of an Indian sari are interpreted here in bold, dramatic wall colours; and the textile's whorls of pattern are reflected in a curly metal candelabra. Let your starting point lead you to a scheme; then work on creating and refining the finer details.

Standing in a fabric shop, clutching a precious swatch of material and searching for something to go with it: we have probably all experienced that feeling of panic when faced with the huge choice of patterns and colours available, and the pressure of that revered and dreaded word, taste.

But there is more to redecorating than successfully composing a scheme in this season's colours. Whatever you choose to do in a particular room will become part of your life for the foreseeable future. Every day you will see the new colours, patterns and textures you have selected and, depending on how successful the whole project has been, be inspired, moved, or disappointed by them. What is more, everyone who visits your home will have something to say, a judgment to make, and most of us cannot help but be affected by that as well.

The more you think about it, the more terrifying the whole concept of redecorating becomes. It is little wonder that so many decorating schemes teeter on the brink of something special, even radical, and then fall back into being safe compositions of neutrals, or white with a splash of colour. But you do not have to compromise. Putting together a scheme is undeniably a creative process and requires certain skills that can be developed and refined. Some basic guidelines will help to smooth the way from the outset, and these are underpinned by a very simple principle.

up at auction, might set you thinking about crisp, tailored loose covers as well as other upholstery styles that you can mix with them. An influence might be infinitely more oblique – the exotic textures of an embroidered Chinese bag; delicate floral imagery on a perfume bottle label; the mix of grey flannel and red wool spied in a fashion magazine. The possibilities are limitless. The key task is to focus on how and where to seek out your single inspiration and to learn how to interpret it in your decorating scheme.

## SOURCES OF INSPIRATION

The most obvious spurs to inspiration are the wider themes we turn to when we decide to decorate – colour, pattern, the proportions of a room and the quality of light. Once you have decided on a particular colour or pattern you have an instant focus. In decorating terms, they are often already captured in a user-friendly form. Fabrics can be touched, and cut straight from the roll; paints can be mixed to order; tiles and trimmings can be bought off the shelf or carefully customized. Key fixed elements such as space and light also need to be considered, planned and utilized in an essentially practical way. Thus, an abundance of sunshine in the dining room might inspire the use of hot Indian shades such as yellow ochre and tangerine; or a little bedroom may automatically call for a delicate mix of tiny patterns and small-scale furniture.

**Above** Use the tones and elements of landscape. The definite, fresh colour seen in this cerulean blue and white sky creates an informal ambience that is further enhanced by casually placed pebbles, and striped fabrics.

It is this. Every decorating scheme should evolve from a single point of inspiration, something that so excites your imagination that you keep coming back to it with a desire to elaborate on it. Everything else – colour, texture, pattern – will follow on from this starting point. The focal point that will provide the building blocks for an entire decorating project could come from any one of myriad sources. You might be drawn to an exquisite document wallpaper in tantalizingly unusual colours, or to a new collection of plain velvets in riotous jewel shades. A curvy little armchair, snapped

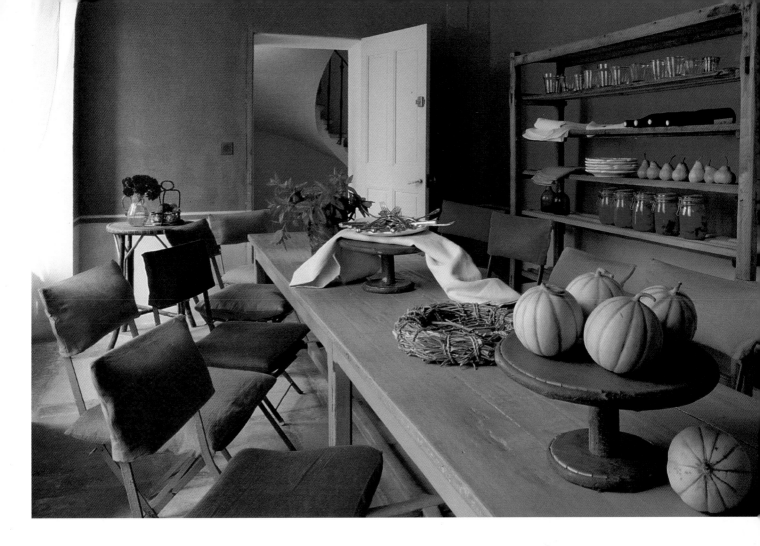

To step beyond these conventional, though valid, beginnings, you will need to open your eyes to new influences. This might simply mean walking into the room to be transformed and scrutinizing it for precious details – the naturalistic curves of oak leaves fashioned into a central ceiling design, pattern swirled into new plaster, the buttons on the back of a Chesterfield waiting to be re-covered. And become alert to more unexpected sources. Mentally list your most precious possessions. Why do they inspire you? Could the surface design of a cracked but much-loved jug inspire a decorating scheme? Are the different shades of colour in an artist's postcard the ones with which to transform your bedroom? There might

be a mood you could emulate. Maybe you have felt uplifted by the sculptural use of stainless steel in a restaurant; or by a descriptive passage in a book.

Train yourself to analyse various stimuli in terms of design, colour and contrast. This exercise is not simply about exploring what appeals, but why, and it will also help you to see how separate components work together. Scrutinize shop window displays; examine the way precious objects are laid out in a gallery; notice the subtle, urban tones and textures of a city street and sky. Look, analyse and respond.

## FINDING A DIRECTION

Show three individuals the same swatch of patterned fabric and they will each respond

**Above** Observe chance colour combinations. Flashes of hot pink, red and lime in a Mexican market place inspire colourful upholstery. Such a scene is also recalled in the colours of a rustic kitchen.

*9*

**Above** Building a scheme. The transition from inspirational starting point to finished room relies on first amassing samples. They help you to refine ideas, to make choices and transform them into reality. Include fabric and paint swatches, and samples of door furniture, trimmings and surfaces. A glass finial may be as significant in the grand scheme as the ultra-chic silk stripes.

to it differently. Remember this as you consider your own chosen starting point. The initial attraction of a fabric may be its texture, unusual colour nuances, or the evocation of precious memories; but there will be any number of ways of interpreting the fabric in a decorating scheme. It is up to you to seek them out. For example, a piece of 1930s large-scale floral fabric could provide the basis for a whole colour scheme that works because the shades already look appealing together on the fabric. But explore other possibilities. Perhaps a floral theme could be developed, using a mix of shapes, scales and colours. Or would the period flavour be more appropriate in your house: an authentic 1930s feel in the drawing room with paint shades and furniture to match? Then again, your fabric may be a temptingly soft, linen weave. Is a textural theme the answer? Keep experimenting until the formula feels right, and always trust your instincts.

## CREATING A SCHEME

There are detailed makeovers throughout this book that show a variety of ways in which to put together decorative schemes, but the basics are always the same. Build on your starting point by amassing as many fabric swatches, paint cards, surface samples, flooring ideas and furniture shapes as you can. Tear out inspirational pictures from magazines, phone or write for catalogues, haunt appropriate shops and take photographs of furniture and accessories that you like. Dedicate a special area to putting them together, be it a table in the room to be decorated, a scrapbook or a display board. Then start to experiment with the different elements that you have gathered: try out unexpected colour combinations, lay unusual textures side by side, contrasting scale, seeing what works and what does not. You will need to consider, at all times, the space that you have to decorate, how much natural light is there in a room, what is the quality of that light and what architectural features need to be highlighted or hidden. Focus on furniture you already have, what you need to keep or acquire, and styles for soft furnishings. Decorating is never just about fabrics and colours, but about weaving them around the bare bones of a room to create a composite whole.

## FINISHING TOUCHES

When we compose an outfit we all, consciously or not, add contrast details; be it a scarlet lipstick with a purple dress, or a jaunty tie with a plain suit. Apply the same idea as you create your living environment.

Any room will be enlivened by little flourishes and highlights, but such details are often neglected in the flurry to finish decorating. You might trace a line of subtle gilding along a moulding; add a flash of brightly coloured braid to a neutral linen curtain, or display striking sculptural flowers in a contemporary vase. Later chapters have plenty of ideas for detailing, so think about where you might add a vital finishing touch to your decorative scheme.

**Left and Below** Few of us have the luxury of starting entirely from scratch. Early on, assess the potential of the furniture that is to stay. Can it be revamped with a cool, contemporary textile or regrouped for a fresh silhouette? But be ruthless, too, and decide what can go. Keep only what is essential or what you really love. In this way you enjoy the clearer space or add revitalisingly new pieces.

# COLOUR

Colour surrounds and inspires us.

Subconsciously, we register and react

to it all the time, but it is easy to

take for granted many of the tones seen

day to day — a passing blue car, the

subtlety of a dusk sky, a pinkish-red postal smudge on an

envelope. Yet, colours demand an instant and very personal

response from every individual. Once it is introduced onto walls

or into furnishings, colour automatically becomes a focal point.

If we have no experience of putting colours together, we may

lack the confidence or worry about using them, in case they are

too bright, do not match, or may slip out of fashion. Yet an

interior without colour lacks personality, so it is well worth

trying to make it work for you.

## SOURCES OF INSPIRATION

A single unusual shade, or a clutch of contrasting colours, can make an irresistible and vibrant starting point. If you have pinpointed the exact source of the colour – perhaps a paint reference on a chart, or a plain fabric – then you are already a step ahead. It is more likely, however, that you will start by searching for something specific to match an idea of a colour in your head, such as 'sky blue', or some tones vaguely remembered from another location. In this event, the most practical option is to look through paint charts or swatches of a plain fabric to see and absorb as many varying hues as you can. This can be a fascinating exercise, discovering just how a single colour can vary from a muted tone to something clear and bright; how pale it can become; and how dark it can go. Take advantage, too, of being able to put contrasting colours together as you flick through the charts and samples. Often a chance encounter will set off a unique combination that really appeals to you.

Although you will find the biggest range of shades in the major manufacturers' colour cards, seek out specialist paint charts, too. Some of them are individually handpainted instead of printed and, as texture can be integral to the final look of wall colours, this can help enormously. Specialist lines are smaller and you may find them more inspirational because the colours are often temptingly arranged together. For example, a page of blues might vary from chalky pale to rich violet tones, or an unfolding strip may reveal some unusual and delicious neutrals. With fewer samples to choose from, you will certainly focus more quickly on the shade you like. Often their names are so irresistible that they grab your attention and allow you to 'see' a colour you may otherwise have missed.

Patterned fabrics offer ample inspiration for colour, too. The beauty of composing a colour scheme using co-ordinating fabrics is that you can see at a glance that different shades are going to work together, whether they are complementary or contrasting, because the fabric designer has already done the

**Above** Intense blue walls cheer a plain room, giving a confident contemporary look. A simple, treated wooden table and chairs now seem modern rather than rustic. Distinct pendant lights and monochrome abstract paintings augment the look.

**Opposite** Hot pink and orange walls become mouthwateringly beautiful when applied in a gentle wash of paint. They make a luscious backdrop to uncompromisingly pretty textiles.

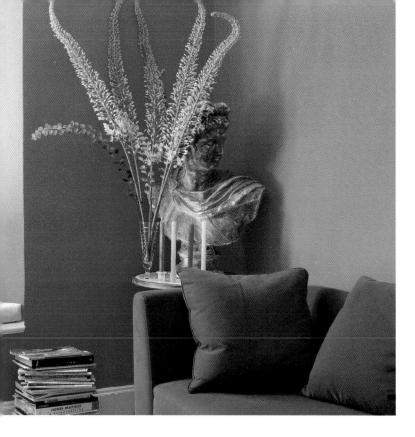

**Left** The combination of a petrol blue sofa and dense dusky pink walls illustrates the essential principle of balancing one strong colour with another.

**Below** Use bright walls to highlight strong shapes. The globe light and monastically styled dining chairs look simply elegant with vivid apple green walls, and a cleverly angled day bed makes an interesting silhouette.

**Opposite** Play up a bold wall colour with a piece of furniture in a similarly strong tone. Dense shades can look fabulously dramatic when teamed with monochrome accessories. The black-and-white wall prints and the aluminium lampshade cut sharply through the cinnamon tones of this modern living space.

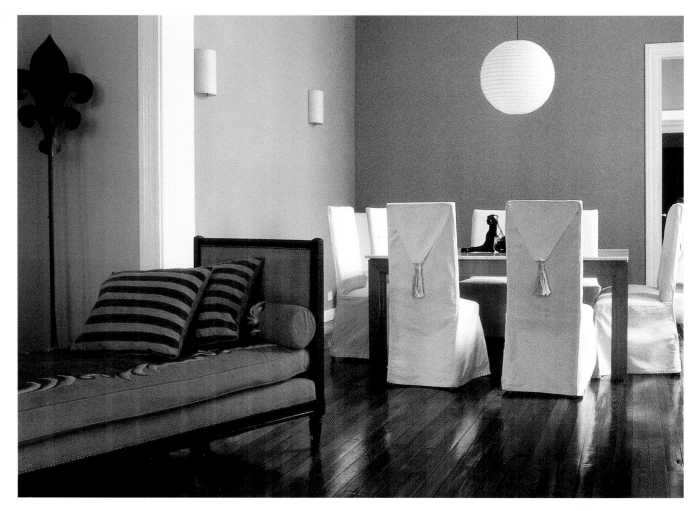

thinking. It is also possible to like a significant colour combination and copy it without using the actual fabric. So, even if you want a plain scheme, it is still worth considering patterned materials and wallpapers as rich initial hunting grounds for colour.

Try to absorb as many colour influences beyond the confines of traditional decorating media as possible while you are brewing a scheme. The richest pickings will come from the world of fashion. This is not just because the trends in interiors and fashion are becoming increasingly linked, but because influences and colours, textures and patterns now move so fast in fashion that there will always be a fresh stimulus. Looking at clothes and accessories, and the way they are styled in magazines, is an excellent way of

discovering how to use accent colours daringly and successfully. Look also to the natural world, at flowers massed on stalls in the street, seasonal vegetables and their varying hues, the ever-changing tones of the landscape. It requires practice to absorb such influences and to imagine what you see translated onto your walls or floors, but the results can be harmonious, surprisingly racy, and deeply satisfying.

Then there are historical colour references. Inspiration may strike when you see a clear and beautiful wall colour in an eighteenth-century painting of a rococo interior, or when you visit a stately home. You might spot a soft, authentic shade on a colour chart of traditional paints. Do not be constrained and think you can only use historical colours if you are bent on recreating a particular period feel in a room. Colours transcend centuries, and a Georgian green will look just as glamorous in a modern, urban factory conversion as in a carefully preserved historic building.

## USING COLOUR : THE CHOICES

Say the words 'using colour' in a decorating context, and some people will assume you mean bright, scary colours like shocking pink or vivid lime. If you do use such colours, you are usually referred to as 'very brave'. You may need a lot of nerve to opt for bold, clear colours on walls or floors, but the results can be stimulating and refreshing. The benefits of using bright shades are manifold. Singing colour is cheerful to live with, and when used on walls provides a wonderful backdrop to show off furniture with unusual lines, or a collection of pictures shouting to take centre stage. It can brighten a dull room, distract attention from bumps in plaster, or simply make a fashionable statement if you are well tuned in to current colours. It can lift an ordinary room into the realms of the extraordinary, particularly if used with quirky modern furniture; but, equally, it gives a new slant on a period interior. And it can be used with other surfaces or textures – a lime-

coloured rubber floor combined with cool stainless steel, say, or scarlet wool upholstery with fuchsia pink walls – to provide those essential contrasts that make such interiors so exciting.

The key to using big blocks of bright colour is first to keep your nerve, and then to stick unswervingly to the principles of balance and simplicity. Strongly coloured walls or floors need at least one other item in the room – an outsize sofa, perhaps, or a bold contemporary rug – that is in an equally heavyweight colour to give essential balance. Painting the walls a bright colour and hoping that it will jazz up all the other existing mid-toned colours of furniture and accessories, simply will not work; they will just look tired and worn. Alternatively, white or neutrals used in quantity are great balancers for vivid shades. With this look, simplicity in terms of few accessories and uncluttered furniture is essential. If you hesitate at using bright colours on all the walls, consider painting just one, perhaps to highlight a pretty fireplace; or turn the entire concept on its head and go for white walls teamed with definitive pieces of furniture painted or upholstered in the strong colours that appeal to you.

Sombre, sophisticated shades, from charcoal to mushroom, plum to sage green, need not be reserved, as some might assume, for historically accurate interiors. Used in the right way, they will look chic and rather worldly, encouraging the fall of natural shadows and contrasts in a room, and promoting a serene ambience. It can take courage to use them, as they are almost as tricky as bright colours to get right. Consider and experiment with them. Their innate subtlety means they can be taken in multiple directions, mixed with pale or rich wood panelling and furniture, mirrors or mouldings brushed with silvery tones, and modern metals in any form. Bright colours can work with them fantastically well, too, as part of the main scheme or as an accent shade – think of a clear, orange sofa ranged against an olive green wall or a grey Roman blind trimmed with red linen fringe. Although white looks good

**Opposite** A subtle scheme using pale, watery mint, lilac, taupe and white promotes a calm ambience that is ideal in a bedroom. Understated accessories – a chrome shade, a tumbler full of lavender – reaffirm the style. Decide what mood you want to create before choosing appropriate tones to enhance it.

**Above** Reassess the power of a deep, sombre palette. Used carefully and dressed up with sophisticated styling, it can elevate a room to new heights. The deep grey walls, cream- and biscuit-toned upholstery and dark wood in this dining room succeed because they are teamed up with well-chosen, tailored loose covers, leopard skin lampshades and the rich depths of pewter.

with sombre tones, steer clear of using it conventionally just for the woodwork, as the contrast will be too great. Instead, utilize the tonal shading of colours on paint charts to decide on your deep shade, then choose a pale version of it, or even a different colour, for the woodwork. And do not forget texture, as restrained shades can be given extra vitality if they are used on different surfaces.

Using colour for contrast, juxtaposition and surprise is one side of the coin. The other relates to light and space. Gravitate towards fresher tones not just because they are 'safe' but because they will perform a decorative function for you. Lighter shades, from white right through to pale lemon and other pastel tints, may create a tranquil space for working or sleeping, and will open up dark rooms. They are also, quite simply, prettier, if that is a look you want to achieve. But they need to be handled just as skilfully, as too many pale shades together can look insipid. Learn to layer pale colours, using different tones to create a discreet but definite framework to the room. You might use up to five tones of a single colour doing this — one for woodwork, another for walls, one for the floor, a fourth for the ceiling, and more for upholstery. It works for colours, and for the whole spectrum of whites, too, which may range from frost to cream. Use this technique in combination with different textures, too, for a harmonious build-up of visual stimuli.

## ACCENTING WITH COLOUR

However carefully composed, no colour scheme will work properly unless it is accented to some degree with contrast

**Above** A room devoted to one colour gains depth from an interplay of textures. Uneven, painted floorboards, soft bedlinen, matt furniture, a translucent blind, with flowers and the soft outline of a shirt, convert a potentially clinical scheme into a pretty one.

**Opposite** Variations of tone in related shades give a gentle wash of colour. The eau-de-Nil cupboards, a pastel blue chair, and a spruce green door frame combine to impart a time-evolved air. Consider ways of using different tones together on a wall or on woodwork, instead of just one colour on each.

or 'detail' shades. The purpose of an accent colour is slightly to dislodge equally balanced colours, to set things on edge, and make them visually more exciting. Equally, colour detailing can be used to draw together apparently disparate hues in a room. It may seem a complex process, but it is something most of us do quite naturally. If you have ever placed a vase of bright green foliage from the garden into, say, a pale blue and white room, you have accented that interior without even realizing it. The vivid colour of the foliage serves to crisp up the softer tones in the interior, and encourages the eye to look at the colours in a new context.

Accenting is about surprise and co-ordination, and it does not have to be a bright colour that does the work. In a room full of strong hues, the accent shade might be a neutral or a wood tone; or in an all-white interior, the accent could be a texture – the sheen of an extra glossy white paint, perhaps. And the accent will not necessarily appear as coloured upholstery, cushions or trimmings. Notice other details that will work for you. Think of book spines all in one colour, mounts in picture frames, the riotous shades of flowers outside the window. You can afford to experiment with accent shades because they are always used in small quantities, so try something even if you think it may not work – and it just might.

## TAKING THE PLUNGE

Composing a scheme around colour requires precision at the planning stage. If you feel confident using crayons or paints, it can be immensely helpful to draw and colour in a rough sketch of how you see the room in your mind's eye. Next, focus on your colour samples of paint and fabric. If that elusive shade of paint remains out of your grasp, turn to the specialists. Experts will be able to mix sample colours for you, and certain fabric houses will custom-weave materials or trimmings to order.

When you are amassing swatches, stray a little beyond the colours you have settled on because you might still at this stage make a surprise discovery. If you are collecting pinks, get some scarlet too. If you are looking for stripes that combine three chosen shades, get one that has a fourth colour as well because that might act as your accent colour.

Check the contrasts a second and a third time, before applying them to your interior, until you are sure that they are going to work together. Look at them physically in the room, at varying times of the day and if possible during different types of weather, because the play of light will, above all else, determine whether or not your combination of colours will succeed. Too much sunshine, and your sunny turquoise will lose its impact; long afternoon shadows, and that chic grey may seem coldly institutional and depressing.

From the tiny colour swatches available it is practically impossible, even for someone with a trained eye, to visualize what a whole room will look like painted a certain colour. Get yourself small sample pots, paint large pieces of wall-lining paper or the back of some leftover wallpaper, and pin them up, to give a better idea of the final effect. Live with them for a while; see what a favourite piece of furniture intended for the room looks like

**Above** Splashes of tangerine, corn yellow and cranberry in an essentially white space enliven the entire room. Cushions are perfect for colour accenting as they are inexpensive and can be changed whenever you are ready for a refreshing new combination.

**Right** Flowers in punchy colours bring real vitality to a monochrome interior. Searing red gerberas relax the otherwise pristine modernity of this room.

**Right** Think which surfaces can be used to unbalance a perfectly poised colour scheme. A purple painted door juxtaposed with another just glimpsed beyond in cherry red, define and characterize a modern white interior. Paler accent colours can be equally strong. A run of honey-coloured, polished wood set against white walls gives a more subtle contrast.

next to a key colour. Remember, bright colours will drain paler shades, and the intensity of all-over wall colour can even throw a sickly cast over paler tones. Equally, what looks like a gentle but definite ice-cream shade on a paint chart, may be swallowed up in a big room and look more like a dull white. You may need to go up a shade to achieve the correct depth of colour. If you have chosen a bright colour as the key to your scheme, and intend to use it for curtains or blinds, drape a sample over the sofa or at the window. What looks like electric blue on a sample board may pale to insignificance when suffused with natural light. You may need to line curtains to retain the essence of the colour, or choose another medium for including that blue in your scheme. Remember, the colour of your curtains, especially their lining, will affect the exterior appearance of your house.

You may think scale is more relevant to pattern than to colour, but considering how much of a colour to use is absolutely vital. Looking at three identically sized swatches of your chosen key colours will give a false impression. Try to gauge the balance of colour by cutting down your samples in proportion to how each will be used – a big piece of the colour intended for a capacious wing chair, say, and relatively smaller pieces to represent cushions. And remember that in a scheme based on plain colours, you can be really adventurous with different textures. Start with textiles, and go on from there, drawing in the smoothness of coloured plastics, the translucence of glass, the wobbliness of handmade tiles or the bite of a raised rubber floor.

# The Acid Test

*A chance combination of wild and subtle shades can inspire a decorative idea in the same way as a single strong colour. This stack of brightly coloured ceramics in crushed plum, grass green and acid sherbet yellow provides the stimulus for a dynamic and experimental colour scheme in a small studio apartment. Their fresh, modern tones open out the space and give this period environment a new, contemporary feel.*

**Above** Keep a watchful eye in shops for colour inspiration: piles of merchandise like these ceramics in colliding colours may form the nucleus of a novel palette.

**Right** Despite its subdued greys and drab curtains, it is obvious that this gracefully proportioned room has plenty of potential.

**Opposite** Dashing, confident colour and a touch of irreverence can twist the period detailing of a room, creating a fresh, contemporary environment.

Slick, fashionable shades are tempting to use. For a season or two they are everywhere, and sensitize the eyes to colours that are addictively vivid but which can be difficult to live with. Using these colours in such a graceful room needs thought. With its elaborate cornicing, floor-to-ceiling windows and

wrought-iron balconies, not all 'modern' colour combinations will be successful. Due consideration should be given to a contemporary colour scheme like this – the combination of acid yellow and plum – to ensure that the attraction will not fade when next season's palette comes around.

Double doors lead straight from the living room into a hi-tech, stainless-steel kitchen in this apartment. The owner's tastes veer towards minimal styling and a contemporary mood, so a vivid colour scheme is ideal. Using a trendy sherbet yellow on the walls means that in years to come the colour can easily be whitewashed out in favour of subtler tones. The more definite shades like deep plum can be kept for upholstery.

## Treading a mid-line

With sharp sherbet yellow walls it is important to use the right colour for the ceiling and the woodwork. Brilliant white is not always the answer as it can look too new and may reduce the depth of colour on the walls. In this room, it would also make the pale marble fireplace look dirty. Instead, a subtle lavender grey defines the woodwork; although this looks quite dark on the paint card, once painted it blends comfortably with white. The colour of the floor is also important. Boldly painted walls need either another strong, clear colour to balance them — perhaps as painted boards, or vivid linoleum — or the right neutral. Here, a green-tinged seagrass matting has been chosen to cover the floorboards because it complements the acid colour of the walls.

After the background 'canvas' is complete, furnishing fabrics need to be chosen. And these are used to introduce the plums and grass green, possibly more acid yellow and, inspired by the woodwork, tones of lavender and mauve. In a scheme dominated by such strong colours, textures will need to work harder if they are to be noticed. The hard-edged stainless steel in the kitchen prompts the use of shiny taffetas and silks; these fabrics, traditionally the reserve of elegant

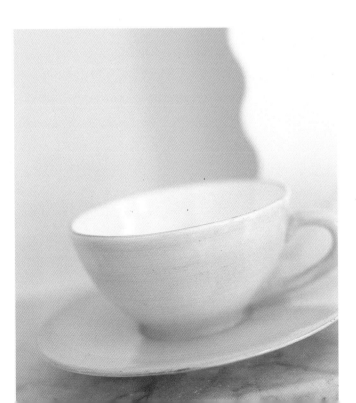

**Opposite** The naturally intense colours of a bunch of flowers are often all that is needed to enliven a carefully co-ordinated scheme. The amethyst tints and vibrant greens of these scabious do not match exactly the plums and soft greens in the room, but are sharper versions of the same shades.

**Above** Clip swatches into a sketchbook, together with snapshots of pieces of furniture in need of a revamp.

**Left** Play with accent colours even after a room is complete. This pale turquoise cup, introduced by chance, looks absolutely right against the silver and citrus background.

drawing rooms, are used here as chic square cushions. To add a softer dimension to this contemporary scheme, classic textures are chosen for the upholstery: striped chenille for the sofa, and chartreuse- and grape-coloured linen to unify two wildly different styles of armchair.

Once it is set against vivid walls, the furniture is thrown into sharp relief. A 1950s-inspired armchair with splayed legs is deliberately picked for its glorious silhouette, as is a modern standard lamp with a crisp, pleated shade. The traditional three-seat sofa looks good in this modern milieu because, instead of being swamped in a conventional cover, it is tightly

upholstered in a fashion-conscious new fabric and teamed casually with a coffee table on wheels. Giving a new twist to period interiors does not simply mean exuberantly coloured walls; it also depends on how you deal with received images of classic furniture shapes.

## Window dressing

Devising successful window treatments in a room awash with brilliantly coloured walls is more complex. Unless the fabric is similarly bold or deliberately neutral, it may dilute the impact of both colours. If the emphasis is firmly on a slick, modern finish, as it is in this room, curtains can be ruled out; blinds will also show off the beautiful windows. As soon as the old drapes were removed from these windows, the room seemed to open out and breathe again. Vivid lime-checked roll-up blinds fit discreetly into each recess and are all that is needed; at night, the working shutters can be drawn across for privacy.

## Metallic highlights

Walls and furnishings in vivid colours are exhilarating, but if strong colour is used everywhere in a room it can become exhausting. Neutrals will cool everything down, and so too will metallics. Think of them as an extra shade in the colour spectrum. Here, the cue is taken from the stainless-steel kitchen, and silvery metals in modern shapes are introduced to build on the contemporary angle. A brushed aluminium mirror surround, a silvery pendant light, a punched steel dining chair and beaten pewter bowls all set the right upbeat tone, while the cool colour and smooth texture of the marble coffee table and fireplace tie in with these metallic highlights.

Some paint colours look so glorious on walls that it is tempting to leave them totally unadorned. However, in this studio apartment, simply framed black-and-white art photographs look chic and understated. If anything, a citrus yellow gives them greater impact than a brilliant white.

**Opposite** However dense and bright fabric shades seem, look at them in direct sunlight to see what happens. A grape-coloured linen armchair is so saturated with colour that it holds its own against the sherbet-coloured walls.

**Above** A dash of warm, rich red in a cluster of anemones offers a stimulating highlight amid the prevailing cooler tones.

**Right** If you dare, pick one shade brighter than your initial choice for windows, because sunlight will dilute its impact. And make what goes into your window box an integral part of the scheme; here, red geraniums give a definite edge to the apple green voile blind.

# Natural Neutrals

*The softest and subtlest neutral hues take their cue from the natural world: a pile of field-fresh mushrooms, sea-washed stones or lichen-covered bark all provide inspiration. When examined, each can be seen to contain its own perfect and complete palette of bleachy shades, from cream to oyster, and from sage to ash. The warmth and depth of nature's tones can be used to smooth a kitchen's modern lines and generate a peaceful, welcoming ambience.*

The ideal family kitchen should act as the cohesive centre of the home, reconciling its different functions with its overall look. It should be sleek and efficient, but it should also be user-friendly for children and easy to transform for grown-up dinner parties. This kitchen has great potential because it is large, long and sunny. A creamy-toned scheme is instantly on the agenda because it will blend easily with the newly laid white oak floor and the original bleached pine dresser (hutch) and built-in cupboard. The appeal of such a scheme lies in its comfort value. Even if you desire state-of-the-art efficiency, this look will take the scary edge off modernity.

A kitchen should be planned to transcend the vagaries of fashion, so that a decade on, there is no sinking feeling that it is wildly out of step with current style. Classic, natural textures, a soothing, 'barely there' colour scheme and pared-down detailing is the perfect solution.

**Above** Give more than a cursory glance to fruits and vegetables. Learn colour lessons from their variegated tones, which sweep from light to dark.

**Left** A large room needs boundaries. Decide at the start on spaces for eating, relaxing and cooking, and balance function with the final aesthetic vision.

**Opposite** A blend of cream and honey tones combine with frosty pastels to create a welcoming family kitchen.

## Natural surfaces

A kitchen's surfaces are all-important. The narrow run of a worktop, the massed cupboards and the tiling all need to tie-in with your chosen colours. Cream paint for cupboards and walls blends well with the fudge tones of the floor. To complement the shiny stainless steel, a charcoal-veined marble as worktop and splashback makes a classic addition. To continue the neutral theme, chrome sockets, opaque glass lampshades and roll-up blinds of white punched cotton are chosen. This is not a style that needs any fussy fabrics.

Kitchens need plenty of storage space for good organization and control. This is one room in the house where there is a constant influx of objects that will interfere with a pared-down vision. This kitchen has enough cupboards to keep less attractive items at bay, leaving the dresser as a focal point for displaying the unpretentious ceramics and garden flowers that work with, not against, the total scheme. More importantly, good storage means that worktops are freed up and can be used to keep practical accessories on hand – Mediterranean-style white platters, a marble pestle and mortar and chrome appliances.

**Above** Functionality and style converge: ultra-smooth marble, vanilla paint, the palest oakwood flooring, and pristine punched cotton combine to provide flawless but practical surfaces. Create a working colour board with hard surface samples, drawing in contemporary silvery accents with essentials like sockets and blind pulls.

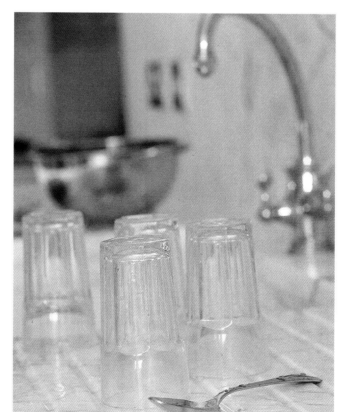

**Left** Match glasses, utensils and ceramics to the overall vision. The enduring simplicity of chunky tumblers takes its cue from the unadorned cupboards and scrubbed wooden table.

**Opposite** Continental chic meets simple country: a shock mixture of styles allows for a family dining space with many faces. With white platters, utility tumblers and casual raffia mats, the chunky wooden table creates a no-nonsense breakfast style.

**Opposite** Palest ice-cream chairs, the rosy blush of hydrangeas, formal napkins and minimalist place settings create, in minutes, an elegant dinner party mood in the heart of the kitchen.

**Right** A slip of window sill, a mantelpiece or the top of a kitchen cupboard all possess display potential, combined with practical appeal. Unassuming china, cunningly aligned and spiced up with a single flower, transforms itself into an engaging still-life.

**Below** Original period features – a fireplace, a cupboard – are seamlessly drawn into the contemporary scheme, by dint of modern styling and a light touch with accessories. A regimented row of wonderfully shaped pots looks fresh and new, while crisp, linen-covered cushions add a touch of unfussy comfort.

## Ice-cream colours

The danger of having a cream kitchen is that it can easily take on a country aspect. Where urban elegance is required, as here, replace too much pine with continental-style chairs in the palest ice-cream colours – frosty blue, pistachio and lemon. These colours have nothing to do with baby blue and sugar pink, and everything to do with new-age style and modern plastics. The two contrasting palettes create a sophisticated edge. In addition, napkins and ceramics in ice-cream shades serve to conjure up a smarter ambience for casual dinner parties.

## Spicy accents

A kitchen needs to allow for changes of mood between one area and another. Efficient stainless steel can predominate at the cooking end, while frosty pastels feature in the dining space. A leather armchair or wicker baskets and pots in nuttier browns can change the pace again, taking the cream and honey tones into a more relaxed vein.

# FABRIC

Fabrics contain numerous elements that can elicit a personal response — the feel, fall, colour combinations, texture, pattern and design. Furnishing fabrics influence the mood of a room,

indicating sophistication or simplicity, reflecting trends, or providing historical authenticity. Equally, a swirl of fabric introduced into a room can, chameleon-like, change its own look to attune to its surroundings.

The fabrics you choose signify your taste and personality for all the world to see, but they are also supremely functional. As a medium that is available in so many forms, fabric offers literally hundreds of choices. And in decorating terms, the selection of one design is not an end but a beginning because it is a rare fabric that is used alone.

## SOURCES OF INSPIRATION

Fabrics offer enormous scope for experimentation. The multi-coloured or patterned features of material provide instant inspiration. Whether it is crisp, unfussy blue-and-white stripes or the watercolour shades and country mood of a finely drawn English rose print, such defining characteristics should set you on a fail-safe path towards a working decorative scheme.

The most obvious inspirations will come from furnishing fabrics themselves, ranging from the latest retail collections to those from more specialist trade suppliers, whose materials will only be available through interior design shops or the designers themselves. You may already have a theme or colour in mind when you start looking but keep an open mind and look at lots

of styles and colours. A surprise find may turn your ideas around and make for a fresher, more uniquely personal result. Fabric retailers invariably push their latest collection, but explore their earlier collections as well. Consider the way fabrics are put together in retailers' sample books. The age of the totally co-ordinated room has gone but most companies include plain-coloured fabrics, small-scale weaves or prints, and wallpapers in matching tones to help you choose. To glean other soft furnishing inspiration, look at how fabrics are styled in advertisements or catalogues.

Exploring alternative sources can be satisfying. They may turn up a unique fabric pattern, and using a fabric unconventionally will make it especially interesting in an interior. Track down theatrical suppliers for different weights of hessian, calico or canvas. Scour dress fabric departments for unusual cloths. Think laterally about other fabric uses. What about school uniform wools and shirtings, or catering mail-order firms that sell linen tea towelling, striped roller towels, and large-scale tablecloths? Search out specialist mail-order fabric companies that deal just with silks, say, in every conceivable weight and colour. A card crammed with swatches might spark ideas for colour or textural combinations.

Losing preconceptions about furnishing fabric and looking at textiles from other contexts is essential. See what other departments in your local store have to offer. Consider if a white drawn-threadwork sheet might look good as a curtain, whether a silk scarf in outrageous colours would look fantastic on the seat-pad of a chair. Look afresh at the clothes shelves. A shift in fashion towards slippery, satin textures might suggest a boudoir feel for a bedroom; or the sight of piles of denim jeans might set you off on the trail of coloured denims.

A specific piece of fabric that has inspired you may not be available in quantity, but a frayed square of Paddington Bear cotton may set off a character-inspired mural in your child's bedroom. You might have a length of handprinted silk in

**Opposite** A single motif unifies a scheme. The combination of checks in varying scales gives an informal air.. Beyond upholstery exploit the potential of tablecloths, napkins or a throw to strengthen themes.

**Right** A fail-safe combination of florals and stripes is linked by delicate tones of lichen and cherry. Ticking stripes next to overblown roses, and crisp Oxford borders next to frilly ones create charming contrasts.

**Above** Sometimes, a bold fabric design is all that is needed to pull together a crisp and punchy look. The white-and-cream linen stripes on the curtains, blind and outsize cushions are allowed to dominate this sophisticated sitting room, while their surroundings are deliberately kept subdued and neutral. Blue delphiniums and a zany zebra rug make brilliant finishing touches.

irresistible colours, bought direct from a textile-design student. Whether it is a remnant, a sale bargain, or your grandmother's old curtains, you must love it enough for the scheme built around it to endure for a number of years.

## FINDING A DIRECTION

At the outset, focus on the physical characteristics of fabric and the interpretations they suggest. Most of us are attracted to patterns because they offer instant visual stimulation. Consider not only other patterns and scales of pattern with which they could be mixed, but also what colour combinations are possible. Is there textural detailing that can be exploited? Is the feel of the material important, the way it gathers in your hand, or does it suggests a certain curtain treatment? Practicality with a touch of frivolity also counts. If you have a young family, it would be wise to pass up silk brocade for the sofa and go for hard-wearing textiles, but a dry-cleanable cushion covered in a sumptuous fabric could add a touch of adult sophistication.

Be on the lookout for fabrics that can be customized. Tea staining and washing will impart a gentle shabbiness to plain and utility cottons, but always do it before stitching, in case the dyeing does not produce the effect you want. Embroider a motif or monogram, appliqué if you have the patience, or trim a curtain or cushion with beading. Insetting a panel of fabric into a contrasting one, pintucking, and patchworking large squares of plain fabrics, are all ways to create more exciting textiles than may otherwise be available.

## CONSIDERING SOFT FURNISHINGS

Fabrics for decorating schemes cannot be looked at in isolation; you must think specifically about their use in soft furnishing terms. The fabric itself may dictate its most flattering incarnation. For example, a large-scale pictorial cloth would look better used in a Roman blind than lost within the folds of a curtain. Or you might need a specific type

**Above** A combination of similarly scaled but unrelated patterns create an informal interior. The lime, aqua and cherry tones in the painterly stripes and Madras check provide colour links. Using scale and colour like this results in a sun-filled kitchen that has a contemporary, just-put-together feel.

**Opposite** This vast and wacky sitting room, with its wild mix of patterns and colour, works because underlying its mad palette of tangerine, grey, sherbet yellow and aqua is a commitment to detail. Broadly striped cushions tie in with a freestanding screen, while the batik print is counterbalanced by the huge geometric shapes in the rug on the floor which in turn are echoed in the abstract painting above.

of material to realize an idea. And many designs, such as paisley, would look equally good in a variety of forms.

For window treatments, consider not only whether a fabric will become curtains, a roll-up or Roman blind, or unlined panels, but also if a grand or simple style is appropriate, what kind of heading you want, whether to use metal or chunky wood curtain poles, a shaped valance or lambrequin. Much of this will derive from the fabric you choose, but consider, too, the context of the architectural style of a room, the total look you want to achieve and what furniture you have. What about trimmings, customized detailing, contrast linings or edgings, voiles, or a separate sun blind?

Upholstery, whether you are looking at fitted or loose covers, is equally crucial. As well as the style, you will need to consider practicalities such as whether your fabrics are designed for heavy upholstery use and

can be washed. Deciding about upholstery always seems scarier than dealing with window dressings, but it offers a lot of scope for individual and creative detailing, and inventive upholstery often grabs more attention than curtains, which may have to compete with a great view. Think about different furniture styles. Do you want upholstered furniture, or loose covers for a more relaxed feel. Will the dining chairs be upholstered in different colours for variety, perhaps with contrasting fabrics on the back and the seat, or maybe you want to concentrate on the details. Think about matching or contrast piping, button, tie or pocket details, or just re-covering the seat-pad of a cosy armchair in a different fabric. Thinking up unusual solutions makes the process fun, not overwhelming. Extend

that frivolity to fabric detailing, too. Cushions, bed-covers, throws, tablecloths and lampshades all have potential for enriching a scheme.

## USING FABRIC: THE CHOICES

Selecting your dream fabric is one thing. Deciding how to balance it with existing features and other component fabrics in the room is more complex. You will have to make choices about mixing patterns, especially in relation to scale, balance and colour; coordinating themes; and building up textures. There may be a clue in your fabric that helps. A floral pattern motif with a background stripe is asking for a relaxed mix of the two elements, but it is not always that simple.

**Opposite** A fabric with an ornate design executed on a grand scale deserves to be seen flat. Textiles stretched onto a frame on a wall give a sophisticated, rich effect that can be expanded by use on a headboard or chair.

**Right** The restrained, neutral palette of this bedroom looks extra chic with its crisply tailored plain fabrics and their contrasting borders.

**Far Right** Drawn-threadwork linens, smooth wool, knobbly herringbone and other textured fabrics could be the starting point of a country theme.

Big, bold patterns, often first to catch our attention, are frequently wasted. Once we have daringly made the selection for, say, curtains, most of us fight shy of repeating it, in case the effect becomes overpowering. But it is a mistake to abandon a statement pattern without a visual reminder of it elsewhere. Even scattering related cushions on it will help anchor it into the overall scheme. Let your bold design enjoy centre stage. Use it right across your upholstered furniture and at the windows for a unifying effect, especially when walls and floors are kept plain. If you want to reduce the impact of the scale slightly, add something surprisingly outsize, a chequer-board floor, perhaps. Or mix it with several other large-scale, but slightly different, patterns – this works excellently with stripes or checks – to provide balance and some extra contrast.

If your fabric pattern is large-scale but not too dominant, for example a toile de Jouy, you can mix it with plain fabrics to keep attention firmly focused on the design; or you could add interest and depth by teaming it with much smaller-scale, companion patterns. There are certain classic combinations that always work – toile de Jouy and checks, florals with stripes – but find your own versions, too. There are few rules for this kind of mixing, although using only one or two unifying colours helps. Experimenting with varying scales is the key. Alternatively, forget about companion patterns, and team your pictorial design with matching, same-scale wall-paper. If such a thing does not exist, use the fabric stretched over the walls, too. It is a braver choice and looks assured and confident.

Consider thematic links where related motifs unify a number of patterns. Such a link can be very obvious, with a large-scale botanical print used alongside smaller leaf-design companion fabrics and antique botanical engravings on the walls. Or the visual references may be more subtle. A combination of fabrics sporting circle motifs with round tables, circular detailing on a chair and a round mirror could draw

**Left** Plain fabrics are easily customized. Translucent, unlined cotton panels, silk-screened with a giant red rose, contrive to look both contemporary and yet pretty in a casual sitting room.

**Opposite** Explore the movement, touch and look of fabric for its innate mood. Dense, rich, rust-coloured velvet contributes to the romantic atmosphere in a room with ochre paint-washed walls and candle-effect lighting. Heavy damask cushions and curtains reinforce the mood.

the whole room into the scheme. Simpler versions might include mixing a number of florals, stripes or checks to create a casual, relaxed look. Colour and scale may be less important when there is a strong unifying motif.

Pattern does not inspire everyone and a plain scheme that relies on texture can be very chic. The textural characteristics of fabrics with their own very subtle patterns are another rich vein of inspiration. Imagine a graphic jumbo cord, plain fabrics with a subtle stripe in the weave, or a pintucked silk; the complex patterns created by a mixture of herringbones of different scales; or bobbly sisal flooring combined with the raised texture of tapestry and the regular, knobbly texture of a rib-knit cushion. Then focus beyond fabrics to add other less obvious patterns: stripes of light coming through a Venetian blind to go with the jumbo cord, say; or the latticed cane of a

Bergère chair to emphasize the close-woven pattern of an Indian gauze. Including flooring here is crucial because carpet, woven fibres and wood create their own very definite patterns. Texture has a sensual quality, too. An entire scheme could be woven around feel-good materials: the soft touch of velvet, fake fur, suede or towelling. Add throws that can be cuddled up to, a footstool to caress bare feet, and soft wool curtains that are both fluid and tactile.

## ACCENTING WITH FABRIC

However much attention you have paid to balance and contrast colour in a heavily fabric-focused scheme, think afresh about accenting. An unexpected flash of coloured fabric is a key option. Your soft furnishing details, such as a contrast lining or buttoning on a chair, could provide it. But contrast patterns or textures make serious statements as well. You can add real verve to a room by introducing a different scale, perhaps with an extravagantly outsize print on one cushion cover; or uplift a restrained combination of matt textures with a dining chair covered in glitzy Chinese embroidery. Accenting can affect the mood of a room. A stark modern interior using crisp new fabrics can be saved from looking clinical by the apparently casual addition of a couple of antique throws.

## MAKING IT HAPPEN

The difference in appearance between a small swatch of fabric and two metres (or yards) showing the whole pattern repeat is terrifying. Take home as long a length of fabric as possible; most shops have returnable samples. Live with your fabric in the room you will be decorating. Scrunch it up at the window, spread it over sofas, tuck it around cushions. Check how it looks in the light and in relation to the architectural character of the room and the floor texture. A simple checked cotton looks great with limed (prickled) floorboards, but less appropriate with carpet. Is the fabric at odds with your existing furniture or will it provide an interesting contrast?

With a large-scale design, a small swatch of fabric is misleading because you cannot see how the pattern works as a whole. You might focus on a single rose in it, only to find that on a larger piece of the cloth the same rose pales into insignificance among a trailing trellis of ribbons. What seems to be a gently rambling pattern repeat may become unsuitably geometric when seen over a large area. If you focus specifically on a tiny motif on a swatch of a fabric with a small-scale design, you may not realize until too late that, spread over a large area like a headboard, the pattern becomes a blur of dots, with crucial colours lost in an unplanned sludge. Also, the play of light can alter the appearance of plain and textured fabrics by diminishing the intensity of its colour; or, from certain angles, failing to highlight an interesting weave pattern.

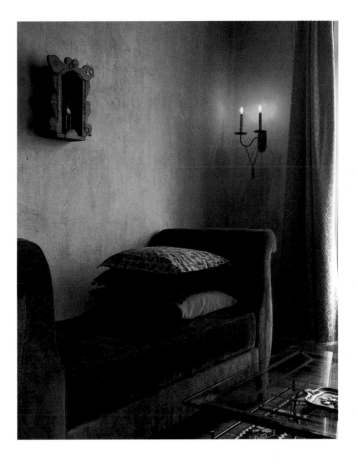

After considering all your curtain or soft furnishing options, it will be time to make specific decisions. Cultivate a flexible curtain maker and/or upholsterer. Make your own sketches, however rudimentary, of ideas you want to try. A professional will be able to interpret a look in practical terms from your pictures or drawings.

It will not be until you have an estimate of how much fabric is needed that you will know how expensive your scheme is going to be. Sometimes, the need to cut down on quantity generates a more inspired result. Your favourite fabric may have to be used only as a broad border on a curtain made of a cheaper plain fabric; or your armchair be made up in hessian (burlap) instead of linen. Such compromises often look more individual. And there is nothing as satisfying as knowing that you have spent less and still achieved ravishing results.

# Classic Pattern

*A classic toile de Jouy evokes the elegance and style of a grand French château. Pictorial and ornate, it demands to be taken seriously, yet its subtle shades inspire prettiness, too. This one, in faded deep purple and parchment, forms the backbone of a large room that combines both a living and dining area. Confidently mixed with smart stripes and opulent textures, this toile de Jouy imparts freshness with a touch of grandeur.*

It is hard to fail with a classic fabric design, a toile or possibly a floral chintz. Invariably beautifully coloured, with a timeless appeal, they are unlikely to fall out of favour because they transcend fashion. Yet you cannot ignore the sometimes rigid style associations that such a classic brings with it. Of course toile de Jouy has the air of a French château, a hint of period living. It is the degree to which you interpret those connotations that will dictate if a scheme is new and original or a mere copy of what has gone before.

This drawing room benefits from plenty of light and suitably grand proportions. As it is both a sitting room and a dining room, the fabrics chosen need to mark out changes in the key areas, while the palette remains tonally strict. A toile offers the scope to do both. It mixes quite easily with stripes, plain fabrics and other toiles, and its characteristic dual tones keep colour choices relatively simple.

**Above** With its purple and dipped-tea tints, a classic toile sets an entire room scheme in motion.

**Left** This Victorian room has plenty of light and good proportions, qualities that have been exploited in this fresh, cool scheme.

**Opposite** The power of a classic design: from a single toile comes a dining room suffused with the romantic air of a French château. Crisp tailoring, distressed furniture and a few detailed flourishes complete the transformation.

**Left** The success of a living room lies not just in its surface detail, but in the way furniture is arranged to promote comfort and ambience. Place seating in intimate groups so that you do not have to shout across the room, and keep side tables realistically close so there is always somewhere to put down a drink.

**Opposite, above** Look out for antique fabrics in specialist shops, sales and markets. A piece of furniture covered in something authentic can be intellectually, as well as decoratively, satisfying.

**Opposite, below** Using ornate fabrics like silks and satins may seem difficult, not only because they are more expensive but also because you may not want too formal a look. The key is to supplement your favourites with simpler linens and cottons, and choose wonderful colours that pull together the whole look. The warm deep purple in the toile is repeated throughout the scheme, shifting tonally to plum and purple, and then to paler silvery mauve.

## A luxurious touch

You can be very grand with toile, or monastically simple. This room finds a midway path by interpreting the ornate French château style with rich, decadent fabrics and by restricting the use of toile to chic little slipcovers in the dining area alone. Too much toile can easily look fussy, and this room needs to be grown-up without being too stiff. The luxury element comes from the texture of the fabrics, rather than their patterns. A sofa becomes invitingly sophisticated covered in a sensual velvet, as does a Victorian chaise longue dressed in an antique satin. Continuing the theme, a modern satin stripe is used on the chair.

These are all formal fabrics and yet they sit happily in this room because they are used simply. Getting it right is vital. Silks and satins frequently feel overpowering because they have been trimmed with grandiose fringing, or because they have

been used in abundant swathes. Here, however, the chairs are self-piped with no extraneous detailing. At the windows, where silk curtains might have swung the balance of style, there is only white cotton lace. This performs a dual function. Not only does it tone down unnecessary grandness, but it allows maximum light into the room.

Carefully matching fabric patterns impart formality, but a more relaxed mix is much easier to live with. Thus, a patterned stripe and a simple stripe, with a plain velvet and an expanse of white linen tablecloth, move the toile a step away from its grandiose feel towards a more original combination, with a touch of modernity. Freshness comes, too, from plain walls in a mixture of cool grey and white, and from floorboards that are sanded and washed down with white emulsion (latex).

Shades of colour, all variations on the two-tone toile, are necessary for uniting this dual-purpose room. To play on the parchment hues would create too antique a feel; instead a shift from cream to palest grey lightens up the whole palette.

**Opposite** Where a single long room has a contrasting function at each end, pay attention to how you divide the two areas both physically and visually. A stately chair in the French style bridges the gap between formal dining area and the prettier sitting area, and its cream-and-plum stripe draws together the varying strands of colour.

**Below** A lean and romantically curved glass jar, crushed-purple pleated ribbon, and a crystal salt dish combine on a stiff white cloth. The contrast of decadence and simplicity gives the dining table a decorative edge.

**Above** The gentle scrolls on the toile find their match on a mantelpiece. Pretty mouldings should be echoed by accessories like decorative painted porcelain.

imparts a time-worn air and looks at ease with toile. A tumbling glass chandelier, though not of the correct period, gives the feel of a château. Think about what accessories can do to heighten the mood. While the dining area is formal, this sitting room aims for a tranquil and relaxing ambience. The portrait of a woman, a floral oil in minty green and pink, scrolled teacups on the mantelpiece, all create an elegant and intimate atmosphere.

On the dining table, essential components of glassware, china and utensils echo the themes of the room in another way. New biscuit-toned floral china cuts through the starchy whiteness of an antique cloth, and simply blown wine glasses contrast with a decorative swathe of pleated plum ribbon. On the table, meanwhile, the colourful potential of fruit and food has been exploited to the full. Vivid purple grapes and dark red wine bring the coolness of the dining area utterly to life.

The deep purple provides the starting point for the other fabrics. Reinterpreted as silvery mauve in the velvet and patterned stripe, and sharpened to plum in the satin stripe, these tones are given an edge when accented with blood-red tulips.

## Fine-tuning the room

Interpret one vein from a particular style, and it will follow a trajectory of its own. The grandness of toile cries out to be paired with French furniture, so cane and wooden chairs, a distressed mirror and an occasional table with a touch of gilding form the core of this room's furniture. But it is so much more a case of borrowing from the look, rather than adapting it wholesale. And you can cheat. A new gilded Louis XIV chair can be made to look aged or, washed in the palest grey, even the most unremarkable mirror frame can be cleverly disguised.

So, in a room that takes at least some of its inspiration from a fabric classic, look to accessories to weave in period elements. Petit-point needlework, on a cushion and a rug,

# Cosy Textures

*The allure of a special fabric lies as much within its weave as in the pattern. A glassy starched linen, crumply waffle cotton, or tough mattress ticking all provide unique beginnings for reinventing a room. The wintry soft wool and ice-blue shading of this throw prompt new ideas about how to decorate a shadowy, low-ceilinged country guest room. Key elements in this scheme are the interplay of a cool colour palette and generous textures.*

**Above** Thick and tactile textiles drape well. Consider them not just for a comforting throw, but as dramatic curtains or a luxurious covering for a fireside armchair.

**Right** This charming cottage bedroom features sloping floorboards polished over centuries, a deep window seat, and a low, beamed ceiling.

**Opposite** The room's principal disadvantage is a lack of sunlight, so the terracotta walls are replaced by planes of cool, light colour.

It is a huge leap from choosing a throw to creating an entire sampleboard ready for action. Analysing a room will provide decorative guidance. As this is a characterful bedroom, with chunky polished old floorboards and bowing walls, mixing the smooth wool throw with cosier country textures will create the right feel. A deeply recessed window means that the bedroom is quite dark. So, although walls painted pale blue-grey will maximize the sunlight, the scheme will also need warming tones to bring it to life. Glancing out of the window on a winter's day finalizes the palette. Red rose-hips, hoar frost and a pale grey winter sky look so glorious outside, it is almost certain they will work within.

Celebrating a country cottage room with classic, rustic motifs and artisan-style furniture seems entirely appropriate. The pastoral scenes on a French toile, teamed with gingham, produce the perfect, timeless mix.

## A soft touch

A bedroom is the one room filled with textiles that do not come off the roll. Sheets, blankets, quilts, throws and pillowslips can be individual handworked pieces and will all contribute their own textures. The scheme in this room is to be done in reverse, starting with the bed. This is appropriate here as the bed is the focus of the room. Curtains come later; the initial search is for soft country weaves. Comforting waffle blankets, a cherry-coloured quilt, sheets in crisp cotton and heavy neutral linen, and finally a rich red plaid throw, all add complementary textures. The crowning glory is a pair of puffy feather eiderdowns, made up in the red-and-white gingham that is central to the scheme.

To give full rein to the glorious mix of textures on the beds, the rest of the room is a simple canvas worked out in three colours. A cherry-red toile de Jouy to match the gingham, heavily woven white linen and canvas, and an ice-blue stripe and check to reinforce the initial colour reference. The pictorial toile would have looked too grand as curtains, so instead it is used in a broad strip on thick country drapes. White canvas for the window-seat cushion reflects as much light as possible, while cushion covers and a chair seat are made up from pale blue fabric.

The walls are washed in sky-blue tones, a paint shade carefully picked from an historical range so that it is in keeping with the period nature of the room. The furniture, deliberately chosen last, is unadorned and rustic, and has been simply painted with white emulsion (latex) to tie it in with the overall scheme. Similar pieces can be found at country fairs.

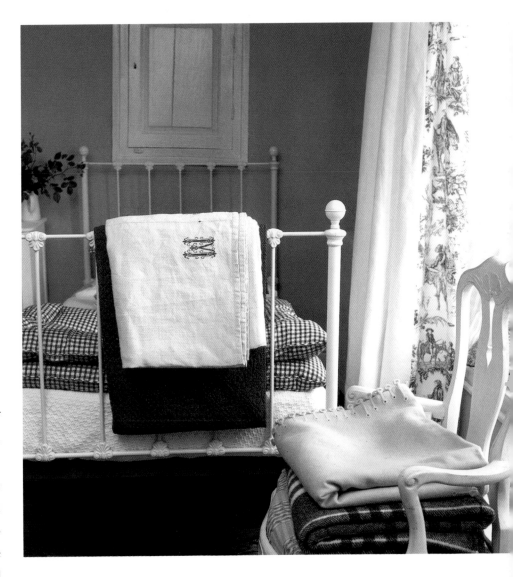

**Opposite** A riot of patterns – gingham with toile, stripes with sprigs – take on a cohesive look if married together within the confines of a strict two- or three-colour palette. For an understated scheme like this, it is essential to mix plain fabrics with patterned ones. Keep to a unifying background colour to hold everything together: fresh white is the key in this collection.

**Above** Thoughtful detailing counts in a guest bedroom. A side chair on which to fold clothes, extra blankets in case of cold, crisp cotton sheets and a vase of fresh garden flowers will all make overnight visitors feel extra welcome.

# Graphic Motifs

*A rose, a bee, a twirling leaf: for every random pattern, there is another*

*featuring the simple repetition of bold, parallel lines. These fabrics are rarely*

*the central players in a scheme: rather, they are for mixing and layering,*

*for the fleshing out of themes and the bolstering of grand designs. Yet*

*this beautiful figured Spanish embroidery contains the kernel of an idea for*

*the dramatic transformation of a light-filled city apartment.*

This first-floor sitting room is broad and sunny with — unusually for a city apartment — two sets of French windows (doors). The apartment had not been decorated for at least a decade, and the room was ripe for a total and radical overhaul. The discerning owners wanted a look that was exciting and modern, as well as being chic enough for entertaining. The French windows give the room a continental flavour, suggesting warm sun and the use of punchy colours. However, a recently acquired slim sofa, in its basic upholsterer's calico, also needs to be brought into this equation. Mediterranean fabrics provide a good starting point for vivid, passionate shades. Beginning with a good selection of fabric swatches all with a Spanish theme, the sofa is re-upholstered in a lavishly embroidered cotton. The bold, regular motif is in keeping with the sofa's formal shape and the warm tones of the stylized flowers can be exploited throughout the room.

**Above** Contrast the formality of a graphic pattern with fluid detailing, like the gentle gathers on a cushion or a soft frill around a chair seat.

**Left and Opposite** The French windows (doors), allowing in maximum light, set the tone for a light and airy scheme. Floral, check and plain fabrics are chosen in equal measures to achieve a harmonious balance, without any one of the designs stealing a march on the others. Likewise, the strong, clear turquoise is balanced with similar expanses of cream.

**Above** Curtains with contrasting
borders look slick and polished
and brighten up plain cotton,
linen or wool. Deep shades
can be contrast-lined, too.

**Right** Create a colourboard
from a single motif by painting
a square of card (poster board)
in each of the shades in the
design. Then lay a sample swatch
of fabric on each card; this will
make it easier to determine which
colour feels right for the walls.

## The right mix

Choosing a colour scheme from a fabric can be difficult.
Here the embroidered flower is made up of a number of
colours from scarlet, plaster pink and turquoise, to cream,
forest green and gold. For impact, the sitting-room walls
need something bold. Forest green and gold seem too
traditional for a fresh, contemporary ambience while, in large
quantities, red is too deep and pink too cloying. Turquoise,
however, is satisfyingly serene, yet at the same time vibrant
and a touch Mediterranean. The floorboards are painted
vanilla to disguise the wear and tear, and to hint at a cool
surface normally associated with hotter climes.

Unadorned cotton fabrics are the focus for the soft
furnishings, as they are understated, crisp and in line with
the plain cotton background on the sofa. In fact, the sofa's
creamy background inspired the purchase of an entire
bolt of calico (muslin) from which emerged flowing full-
length curtains and a re-upholstered formal French antique
armchair. Use plain fabrics with care in a formal setting,
so that curtains do not end up resembling
dust sheets, and newly minted upholstery
does not look as if it is still waiting for a
revamp. These drapes have been cleverly
customized with ties and edging in a
contrasting red cotton. A fringe of contemporary hessian (burlap) enlivens the
brushed-cotton stool.

Although plain fabrics and a single
pattern look good, a splash of traditional
check in a modern turquoise gives the entire
room a razor-sharp finish. It reiterates the
contemporary angles of the sofa and echoes
the weave of the coir mat. It also transforms
an ordinary armchair into a covetable piece
of furniture with its crisp, box-pleated cover.

**Opposite** Less is always more:
relaxed, minimal accessories
give the right contemporary look. A
spindly gilded lamp with a
tall coolie shade, wobbly ceramics
in palest cream, and unframed
oils casually propped against
the mantelpiece allow the colourful
walls to sing out without distracting
the eye. Vivid greenery or massed
flowerheads all of a kind look
stylish in a modern interior.
Lime and red provide this room's
principal accent shades.

# FURNITURE

Grand or simple, each piece of furniture tells its own story. It is a composite of a designer's inspiration, cultural influences, its material make-up, and function. The older it is, the more messages and memories it carries. As its physical components become uniquely mellowed by wear and tear, it takes on more of a character of its own. Colour and light are responsible for the natural ambience of a room, but the furniture placed within it stamps a personality. A piece may be chosen for its shape, materials, its historical resonance, or to reflect a trend. Equally, a piece may choose us by being handed down through generations, or by fulfilling a practical need. However you acquire it, exploit its potential. If it has none, have no qualms about starting afresh. Beautiful furniture is often the key to a beautiful room.

## SOURCES OF INSPIRATION

It is rare to start a decorating scheme without a single stick of furniture. A room filled with brand-new pieces lacks the emotional attachment most of us have for furniture that we have lived with in other settings. Weaving a scheme around constants should not be a chore but seen as a helpful structure for developing ideas. The more you consider what you have in a positive light, the more likely it is that a piece will suggest an entire decorating scheme. And if a multiplicity of paint colours and furnishing fabrics makes it hard to choose, turn to furniture as a starting point.

Suddenly, instead of colours and patterns, you are thinking in terms of hard surfaces – wood, metals, plastics – and shapes, so there is less worry about what matches what. The principles remain the same. But the focus is different. A set of 1950s kitchen chairs in sweet candy colours might set you off in a kitsch direction, or provoke a colour scheme. Style and historical influences become more significant and can be interpreted more literally. A curvaceous French country armoire may set you on the road to a combination of rustic furniture and Provençal cottons. Or the elongated, strict lines of a Regency sofa may become part of an historical transformation. If they are there, exploit more subtle connections. A swirly pattern on an etched glass cupboard front might set off a motif-led scheme. If the single most stunning feature of a piece is its gigantic size, go with that, too.

Antique shops, flea markets, garage sales, salvage yards and auctions are brilliant hunting grounds for every type and style of furniture. Start to define and refine your taste if you do not already have a specific style. This is not about getting good value or making an investment, although they are relevant, but about finding things that please and inspire you. Consider the clear, graphic lines of modern furniture, in shops and magazines. You might not want to live with such trendy pieces but their new mood might cause a subtle change of direction.

## CONSIDERING FORM

Shape and size determine the way furniture works in a room; they are constants that cannot be changed. Start by considering the positive aspects of the shapes; which pieces work in harmony; and whether one of them, perhaps a wing chair, has such a strong outline that it deserves to be made a focal point. Think about how you might emphasize it. Perhaps place it centrally, where it can be admired from different angles, or range it against a wall painted in a defining colour. You might even highlight the lines of a tightly upholstered piece with plain fabric and decorative studding. Do not restrict your

**Opposite** Look beyond the received function of a piece of furniture. Its form and spirit may suggest an alternative use. Far from looking drab, school chairs have a strong, simple outline that sits well in a fresh, minimalist scheme with pale wood flooring and white walls.

**Right** The more individual a piece of furniture, the more it has to contribute to a scheme that combines styles. The freehand outline of this painted headboard has rustic overtones and looks good with the casual colour-washed walls, simple bedlinen and stone floor. Yet, the combination of its random curves and an eclectic collection of bedside treasures gives the room a quirky look that transcends traditional country style.

thoughts to one room. Think about your furniture throughout the house and do not hesitate to swap pieces around to get a good balance. If all the shapes seem disparate and fail to make a great statement, seek to unify the furniture in some way. Loose covers on a diverse selection of armchairs and sofas in a single fabric and style work wonders. Likewise, use a paintbrush on junk-shop finds and less valuable pieces.

Size should be worked with and played up, rather than despaired over. It will always be an issue if you live in a small space and have too much to cram in. Keep only furniture you really love or that is indispensably useful. If any piece is too big for its designated space, abandon any preconceptions you may have that a room needs a certain amount of equally spaced furniture in it. A tiny room with a wonderful, large bed and clothes hanging decoratively from pegs will be more stimulating than the same space stuffed with a smaller, nondescript bed and a chest of drawers. If you have a large room with little furniture, think about arranging it in groups in order to fill the space, paying attention to scale so that varying heights distract attention from small proportions. Or, perhaps you might invest in one huge piece that will dominate the space.

Look afresh at the textures, colours and properties of each piece of furniture. If a table is grand and made from a beautiful wood, it should become a focal point. But a crumbling and faded paint surface or scratched gilding can be appealing, too. You might want to highlight an old chair by collecting around it several similarly 'distressed' pieces – a mirror, an occasional table, a lampstand. If none of your pieces has a special texture, consider faking it. Add contemporary laminate to an old table, or gently distress a new pine cupboard with a paint effect. Your choice of fabric pattern may change the character of upholstered furniture. Modern or utility fabrics give an unusual twist to traditional shapes, and a classic chintz on a space-age shape will look innovative.

**Above** Cracked and peeling paint, with its glimpses of partly exposed colour, can itself be the inspiration for a decorating scheme. A simply furnished bedroom becomes a restful retreat with only a rustic armoire and iron bedstead.

**Opposite** Look for elements that will soften the hard edges of a modern interior. Chairs of shiny white plastic with tubular-steel legs might have had an overly cool influence in this contemporary kitchen, but the matt grey linoleum floor, filmy curtain and wooden table all help to diffuse any hint of clinical modernism.

## CONSIDERING FUNCTION

Furniture is essentially functional, however gorgeous. Think how a room will be used and what wear and tear individual pieces might receive. The function of a room may demand practical features from its furniture, such as storage space, or a large work station in a home office. Consider alternative uses for your existing furniture. Would the dining table be better used as a desk, or the bulky wardrobe in the spare room be more useful, and look more spectacular, as a food cupboard in an unfitted kitchen? Add inventive detailing so that it is beautiful to look at, too. Think laterally about the received use of each item. A large mirror makes a stunningly original headboard, or a one-off antique dining chair can become a pretty and serviceable bedside table. But if the shape of a piece of furniture overshadows its function, locate it where it can be seen to the best advantage.

## USING FURNITURE: THE CHOICES

Furniture is a powerful decorating tool and very different effects can be achieved simply by unifying or juxtaposing the various pieces. Linking factors are easiest to work with. You may already have started the process unconsciously by combining furniture of a certain historical period simply because you like the way it looks together. A collection of modern pieces, each by a different designer, might share translucent plastics in indulgent colours as their common denominator, and other shades and textiles could provide more links.

The visual tension arising from unusual juxtapositions of elements that create surprise and stimulation is easily engineered by mixing disparate styles of furniture. But do not make odd combinations just for the sake of it.

Mixing grand and simple furniture also offers potential for altering mood. Introduce a weathered garden chair into a sitting room to challenge too formal a look. Connecting it visually to something else in the room, perhaps an equally battered metal chandelier, will help to anchor it in the scheme. Experiment with a contrast of fabric styles on upholstered furniture. You could use a cheap lilac cotton duck on real Louis XV dining chairs, thus introducing a lighthearted element into a formal setting. Create a more casual feel by the way furniture is placed. Prop rather than hang large mirrors; push a lovely sleigh bed into the middle of a bedroom. Always try to mix furniture to look as if a room has evolved naturally.

## ACCENTING WITH FURNITURE

Unless a very modern or rustic style has stripped a piece of furniture to bare essentials, most pieces have elements that can be teased out and highlighted. Discreet little legs on upholstered furniture can be painted a brilliant colour for extra zip, or the back of a glass-fronted display cupboard might be wallpapered in an indulgently patterned design. Such accent details can send subtle shock waves through an otherwise unified scheme. Accenting can be kept as simple as a contrast texture or shape, such as using a square brushed-steel mirror to break up the soft curvy lines of a room dominated by upholstery.

**Above** Traditional furniture revitalized with creative upholstery can radically alter the look of a room. Classic Louis XV chairs, painted mint green and covered in a saffron- and cranberry-coloured floral print, look quite at home in a period interior, while bringing to it a light touch of humour. Consider which pieces of your furniture could be transformed, and take risks.

**Opposite** A piece of furniture can be customized to disguise its shortcomings, or to give it an individual, quirky new look. This bleached wooden cupboard has been revamped with the addition of rope handles and studded metal panels. Save customizing for the final stages of redecorating a room, so that your detailing can tie the piece into your scheme.

## MAKING IT HAPPEN

Unless you have been blessed with an extraordinarily vivid imagination, you will have to shift your furniture around to discover what works best. Redecorating a room is a marvellous opportunity to consider the space afresh because the existing order will already be disturbed. It could also be the time to jettison any piece that does not work. If possible, take everything out of the room, and reintroduce it piece by piece. You might realize that the two sofas you had facing each other give more scope for separate task areas placed back to back. If furniture is your decorative starting point, decide what colours and textiles work with it. When you are putting together your colour-board, include photographs of the key pieces of furniture, with measurements, so that you can see how the various elements will work in unison.

Inevitably, you will want to search for at least one new piece of furniture to build on a theme or to replace an abandoned article. Knowing your sources is essential. Visit and revisit shops and auctions, and eventually something will catch your eye. If you are looking for a specific period piece, find out who in your area specializes in that type of furniture. Consider reproduction items and mix them judiciously with authentic pieces. The 'classified ads' in interior design magazines are a good source of unusual or specialist furniture. Most furniture shops that make to order can adjust a sofa design to the size you require; will elongate a table to your dimensions; or make whatever you want in a different combination of woods. Working with a furniture designer on a unique piece is not necessarily ruinously expensive. If you see a one-off antique piece that is just right except for its colour, size or price, photograph it, and then find a craftsman to make it. Consider buying furniture from second-hand shops and repainting, recovering or adding unusual details, such as wheels on a coffee table, or sanding a cheap piece of pine furniture and painting it a cool, matt colour.

**Opposite** The furniture in a room will affect its look far more than the colour of the walls. Always consider scale and proportion as well as style. A formal arrangement is saved from stuffiness by the inclusion of both fitted upholstery and relaxed, contemporary loose covers.

**Above** A gloriously proportioned wardrobe from a more opulent age need not look out of place in a small house. Keep other elements to a minimum, colours pale, textiles plain, and let the ornate piece become the centre of attention.

# A Flea-Market Find

*An antique chair, carved and painted, exudes a feeling of frivolity.*

*The curvy legs and nipped-in waist are suggestive of feminine charm,*

*while the faded gilding hints at the decadence of a lost age. Placed*

*in a high-ceilinged bathroom next to the sweeping curves of a roll-topped*

*bath, it signals the starting point of a glamorous transformation,*

*where the richness of gilding and the promise of luxury collide.*

**Above** The appeal of an antique piece of furniture is multi-stranded. Explore its shape, make-up, style and period for the chance to develop a decorative lead.

**Right** Equipped with the beautiful basics of a generous roll-topped bath and pedestal basin, combined with lofty proportions, a bathroom can reinvent itself time and time again.

**Opposite** Understated peach walls and a gleaming wooden floor give way to a wash of lilac and touches of gilding for a glamorous, feminine revamp.

Tiled and modern for a short, sharp sluice, or a temple of indulgence for hours of pampering – a bathroom can be many things. With its sash window, gilded armchair and screen, this bathroom was perfect for a romantic transformation, but its parchment walls and dark floorboards gave it a gloomy air.

The Parisian chic of the gilded chair conjures up visions of a vast apartment with French windows (doors), marble floors, lace curtains and a hint of perfume. But to avoid a clumsy pastiche, this look should be adapted, rather than copied. Rich, dark shades are far too theatrical; instead combine gilt with serene, pretty tones – eau-de-Nil, melon and palest lilac – for something that is refreshing yet decadent. The lilac on the walls means

that the chestnut floorboards do not fit in with the scheme. The radical decision to lay faux black-and-white marble tiles clearly sets the scene for a Parisian-style bathroom, but with thoroughly modern plumbing.

**Above** A self-indulgent bathroom calls for heady perfumes, luxurious lotions and dreamy, scented candles. Remove favourite products from more urbane packaging. Decant brilliantly coloured oils and bubble baths into antique glass bottles, pour bath salts into crystal bowls and keep less beautiful essentials firmly behind a cupboard door. A gilded soap dish and an etched glass toothbrush holder will transform everyday ablutions into something special.

**Opposite** For the ultimate, tactile bathroom, start by assembling fabrics in place of tiles, trimmings instead of taps. Abandon preconceptions about what can and cannot be used. Sheeny textures, airy voile, smooth, pure cotton and a dash of bobbly braid lie at the heart of a decadent, comfortable bathroom retreat.

## Salon style

The secret to an indulgent bathroom is to sort out the behind-the-scenes practicalities first. There is nothing romantic about water-marked satin or damask wallpaper lifting from the wall. Think about surfaces. Floors need to be water-repellent and fabrics splash-resistant; you do not need to have tiles, but marble splashbacks and painted walls are better than wallpaper, which has a tendency to peel. Good heating and ventilation are also essential.

Choosing the perfect shade of lilac paint sets the tone. Classically pretty shades, spreading through the spectrum from lavender to rose, have a surprising variance. There is no such

**Right** Use soaps for dashes of dense, brilliant colour. Gather them in a glass bowl and use them as ever-changing accent shades.

**Below** A chair and plump cushions to relax against take the bathroom to new, indulgent heights. Fluffy towels, a heated towel rail on which to warm them and a velvet dressing gown are the ingredients of the perfect bathtime treat.

colour as pure lilac; instead versions range from blue and pink to grey. What may seem like a true lilac on a paint swatch can look overpowering as a test patch on a wall. You will find a pearly grey lilac has a fresh, light feel to it. White woodwork would look too bright with all the gilded and marbled surfaces. So experiment with alternatives, looking through the palest pastel shades. Here, an unlikely but beautiful whisper of plaster pink eggshell enhances the mouldings and the bath. For a grandiose flourish, the sides of the bath can also be painted in gold.

Luscious textiles are at the heart of a sensual bathroom, though sheeny cottons are preferable to real silk, which can be marked and spoiled by water. The armchair and screen are lifted from shabby chic to contemporary baroque with a fine rib-cotton upholstery in vibrant lime and amethyst. Provided there is an efficient screen at the window, such as a blind or opaque glass, curtains can be used to maximum effect. To achieve a sophisticated salon style, this Roman blind has been made from an embroidered antique linen sheet, and a filmy voile curtain is draped elegantly over a pushback. Lace panels or printed voile are also excellent bathroom fabrics, and a skilled blind-maker will be able to stiffen them gently while retaining their translucent quality.

If there is plenty of room, a bathroom can also accommodate comfortable furniture that will allow you to relax. An armchair, a side table to hold a drink and an armoire crammed with towels and scented linens all turn a practical room into a glorious retreat; you could even create a dressing room if you have the space. But pay attention to style. The select cluster of gilded furniture in this room is enough; adding more pieces would destroy the equilibrium of the look. Instead, a marble-topped side table, a curly

**Left** A simple length of voile, trimmed with bobble fringe and artfully draped, creates a luxurious new look. Experiment with other textiles in the bathroom. An antique linen sheet, clipped in front of a practical, clear shower curtain, looks infinitely more inviting than the squeaky plastic alternative.

iron towel rail, a metal wall sconce and a rose-carved painted mirror continue the mood of decorative, indulgent treasures, gathered together for their antique appeal.

## A modern twist

A period look, however lightly reinterpreted, needs a contemporary edge. Some rooms glory in the mix of antique and modern furniture, but the contrast is much more subtle here. Slick cosmetic packaging — silvery canisters, and cool, conical-shaped bottles — look stylish, as do fresh white towels trimmed with zingy lime. Pretty colours like lilac need acid overtones to define them as fashionable rather than prissy. The lime bobble fringe on the curtain and the startlingly bright lime lozenge soaps, mixed with brilliant turquoise and amethyst, all stop the bathroom from looking too pretty.

A decadent, decorated room benefits from plain and simple undercurrents. The smart black-and-white chequerboard flooring balances the gilded splendour. But so, too, does the crisp monochrome cotton in a Swedish floral print, which has been used to upholster the little gilt chair, and as a scatter cushion on the giant Baroque armchair. Used judiciously, black and white are great equalizers, toning down colour and injecting a little restraint.

# POSSESSIONS

*Favourite things, possessions and treasures frequently have no other purpose except to impart immense pleasure. These are the objects we might momentarily hold or glance at to recharge a memory or appreciate an aesthetic quality. It is human nature to surround ourselves with things we love. And precious need not mean expensive. Too often, such treasures only come out of their boxes at the end of the decorating process to be fitted into the scheme instead of being part of the whole. They are often muddled up with out-of-date accessories, disliked presents, and mistaken buys. So, be clear about what you do love. Does it tell a story, or does it inspire you? Does it impart colour, or is it quirky or pretty enough to become a central focus in a room?*

## SOURCES OF INSPIRATION

Do not assume that as soon as you start looking, objects you have had around for years will mysteriously reveal a secret side bursting to be exploited. It is not that simple. Exploring favourite things for a decorative starting point is more a lateral way of thinking; it should be fun and slightly frivolous. Search through cupboards, look afresh at ornaments and pictures, reconsider pictures you have not had framed, cracked china and family heirlooms. A pattern with inspiring colours on a faded eiderdown may cry out to be part of a shabby chic style. This is more a process of looking at what is around you over time, whether at home, in a shop or at a village fête, and learning to see hidden facets that can be drawn out and developed. Hone your taste so you are able to analyse and react instinctively, having the confidence to buy that chance find.

Think, too, about the concept of a possession. It is not necessarily a decorative object or an ornament. A square of translucent blue soap, clear and perfect, sitting on a chrome

**Above Left** A favourite set of prints can set the style of a room. A group of images in identical frames and hung in a tight block look impressive as they give the illusion of being one big picture.

**Above** Ideas for customizing a display cabinet arise from the nature of a collection. Here, porcelain has suggested an outsize scallop on open shelving. Chinoiserie vases prompted chair slipcovers in green-and-white toile; and the abstract motif of rosy sprigs on the plates is reflected in a cotton lawn cloth.

## USING POSSESSIONS: THE CHOICES

The nature of precious things is as diverse as their owners, but as a general principle, consider your treasure in terms of colour, texture, shape and pattern. To see familiar items afresh, take them out of context, away from where you are used to seeing them, and muddle them up on a table. If a picture appeals and the frame does not, discard the frame and let the image stand alone. Regard everything with a gimlet eye, and put aside anything you do not love.

Items that are intended to please visually — paintings, decorative china, a needlepoint cushion — can be interpreted in much the same way as, say, the designs within a fabric. Consider the myriad strands of pattern, theme and colour. It will be your own private joke to include the original item in the finished room. Few will guess its importance as an inspirational starting point, but you can still enjoy the connection, and the object.

The process will be utterly different if your inspiration is more abstract, items culled from nature or an autumn walk, such as a collection of pearly shells. You might interpret these things literally by devising a colour scheme that reminds you of the beach, the changing light, the sandy textures. Or you might concentrate in a more abstract manner on the texture of rough seed pods and twisted branches picked up in a forest. The resulting decorative scheme may only be subtly linked, displaying a penchant for dark woods, knobbly textures, and a more casual placing of furniture. The mood you remember from that autumn walk will always be uppermost in your mind when you sit in that room, and that is what counts most.

So possessions can hold the key to a direct colour scheme; or they may influence the look of the room subtly. They can take centre stage as a stunning focal point. Perhaps you have a richly framed portrait, your favourite possession both emotionally and visually. Of course, you may take its colours and weave a scheme around them. Perhaps using contrast

dish, holds a glimmer of inspiration for decorating a bathroom using cubist shapes, transparent surfaces and cooling aqua colours. A bowl on a kitchen shelf, crammed with rough string, manila envelopes and household candles may hold the essence of your next kitchen scheme. Try putting together a collection of colours and textures that please and stir you.

Inspiration for displaying possessions may arise from something as obvious as visiting museums and art galleries, where the sole purpose is to show an artefact to its best advantage. Look at the space around a picture, the way it is hung, the grouping of objects. Can this be reinterpreted at home?

as a means of highlighting it. Somewhere in the picture there may be a flash of unexpected colour that could be used on the wall where it will hang. Or you may choose barely-there shades and matt textures, so that the room effectively becomes a blank canvas for one, or several, pictures. Equally, consider ways of displaying the portrait to direct attention to it. Hang it centre stage, alone over a bare mantel-piece. Or work out where a significant shaft of sunshine falls and hang your picture in its own natural spotlight.

Collections with a common theme, or linked visual appeal, can also spark off a room scheme. They might be faded, antique finds lovingly collected over time – handpainted plates,

wooden shoe lasts, or antique maps. Or your tastes could be more contemporary and transitory, changing from one month to the next, from a set of a particular artist's black-and-white postcards to a huge glass bowl filled to the brim with autumn leaves as the season turns. Think how best to use and highlight your collection. You could develop a theme by searching out a map motif fabric, painting the walls in parchment shades, and hanging maps for maximum effect. More subtly, a single handpainted rose on one of your plates might loosely connect with a pretty chintz for a sofa, or a dusky pink for the walls. Or if your collections are likely to change often, then deliberately opt for neutrals

**Opposite** A favourite possession may have only a subtle and almost indiscernible link to the finished scheme. Minimalist cylindrical glass vases inspired this worldly scheme, with its strong interplay of parallel lines and neutral colours.

**Right** A painting can inspire a fresh new scheme. Analyse the colours used to see why they work together. The tonal variations, texture of brush-strokes on canvas, and the lavender blues in this painting have all been alluded to in the handpainted canvas chair covers. The yellow greens are picked up in a bowl of fresh pears, and the neutral tones repeated in the bleached wood of a contemporary table and the sisal floor matting.

or monochrome shades with few distracting patterns, which will allow for that transitoriness. Deep, pale wood picture frames can hold shells one week and sheets of old music the next; tall glass vases can show off textured collections of ribbon or string; a low, simple shelf running right around the room is ideal for displaying anything from new snapshots to treasures from a trip abroad.

The final style of a room is inextricably linked with the grouping of favourite objects, whether you have decided to take your decorative inspiration directly from those same objects, or whether you are putting them together right at the end. Tap into the current vogue for simplicity.

If you cannot decide whether to set out an entire collection of creamware jugs or just the most beautiful one, restrict yourself to the latter. The calmness of one may set you thinking about trying out a clutter-free environment, with barely-there colours and minimal furniture. The way you display things will also dictate the ambience and finished look of a room, be it casual or chic. Think about your natural style. Do you prefer a just-put-down cluster of precious objects; or is symmetry important to you? The latter will be more in keeping with a designed, ordered environment and decorative style. Cross barriers and try out each look to see which feels right.

## THE PRACTICALITIES

Favourite possessions deserve to be admired, not just by you but by friends, visitors and family. So, do not distance your favourite things by hiding them away in glass cabinets or high up on shelves. Most rooms have architectural features which should be considered first, from a deep window sill to a mantelpiece, an alcove to a picture rail. Display things where they can be seen close to or where they can be picked up and admired. If you do need to devote furniture to display, keep it simple. A low tabletop, an open-shelved cupboard, or a sturdy wooden chair frequently look more casual as vehicles for display than do purpose-built cabinets or shelves. But, think practically, too. Are children going to knock things off; does that same low tabletop also need to hold newspapers, or drinks?

An important possession may have dictated the entire layout and scheme of your room, but think also about ways to enhance all the smaller objects. Tricks include gathering coloured glass in front of a window to glow in the sunlight; or giving significance to family snapshots by framing them identically and grouping them together on one wall. Instead of hanging pictures from hooks, trail them from long velvet ribbons, or industrial chains. Cram pebbles from the beach into a shallow glass bowl filled with water to highlight their natural hues.

We can deliberately style special things in a room to get the look we want. Once the decoration is complete and furniture is in place, gather together all your accessories and experiment with them. Prop up pictures on a mantelpiece; arrange unexpected combinations of old and new; clutter a surface, then take everything away except a vase of flowers. Does a lack of things seem clinical or is it a pleasant relief? Live with your new arrangements for a while. Tinker with them until they look right. Displays will be seen afresh if altered from time to time. Remember that less is often more. Too much clutter can kill a carefully thought-out scheme. And the more space left around one special object, the more dramatic its impact will be.

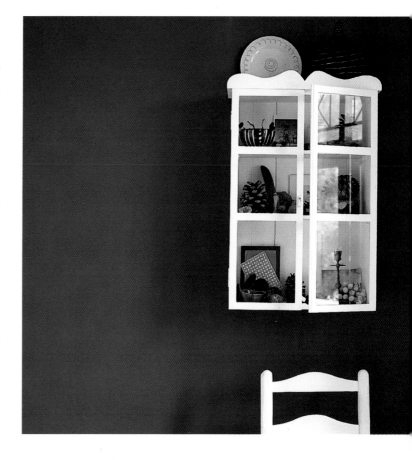

**Opposite** Focus attention on a large or conspicuous item by giving it lots of space, as if it were on display in a gallery. This whimsical bird cage has a wall to itself, with furniture and styling around it kept to an absolute minimum.

**Above** A glass-fronted cabinet, filled with favourite things, needs to be accessible, so that everyone can enjoy the items within. Leave one of the doors enticingly open, as if inviting closer inspection. Keep the display relaxed and random, changing the objects from time to time. Think about focusing attention on the cabinet. The contrast of a white-painted frame set against a midnight blue wall makes this one instantly attractive.

# A Chic Fashion Accessory

*A decorative fashion accessory — whether an impulse luxury buy or rediscovered in a closet — can inspire in unique and surprising ways, not least because it is so often rich in glamour and detail. Subtly shaded and finely stitched, this pair of soft kid gloves from a Paris flea market suggests simple elegance, smooth textures and a lavender-grey colour palette — just right for a city drawing room in need of a decorative fillip.*

These beautiful gloves offer inspiration in three directions. Their sophisticated colour can be the starting point for a palette of greys of varying hues — colours strong enough to make a statement, but not so dark as to be austere. Their elegance and antiquity can be matched with sympathetic furniture styles and ornate accessories. And finally, the soft sheen of the leather, combined with its top-stitching, highlights a need for sensuous, indulgent fabrics. These are the beginnings, but it is necessary to take into account the room itself — in particular its day-long brightness and the beauty of the original window shutters. It is important, too, not to ignore the potential challenge of changing existing features — how to deal, for example,

with the honey-coloured floorboards which are at odds with a silver-toned palette. Finally, consider any large elements that you choose to retain. Here a Biedermeier sofa is intended as a focal point in the room.

**Above** The grey of a pair of gloves is reinterpreted for a room scheme in paler tones of dove, pearl and lavender.

**Opposite** A barely there, neutral shade – like grey – is as valid a starting point as splashier colours. For more depth, explore neutrals in terms of light and dark tones.

**Left** Tall ceilings, original window panelling and good natural light give this room a head start, as there are no obvious flaws that need to be disguised.

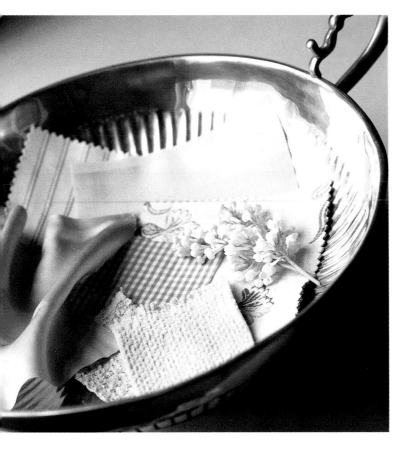

## *A tone on tone palette*

To use the grey of the gloves as an exact colour reference would almost certainly have resulted in too shadowy a colour. Instead, pale grey paint for walls and woodwork sets the scene, selected from shades of antiqued white rather than proper greys. Now the palette needs fleshing out with fabrics: some luxuriously silky in order to add sophistication, and others with a textural twist to add bite to the one-colour scheme.

A chic, silvery crepe satin is ideal for draped window swags and two paler silky stripes sit well as cushion covers and upholstery. Alongside the crepe satin, two textural crunchy matt cottons act as a foil: one to line a tailored throw, the other to make into a second set of cushions. Although this completes the interplay of grey tones, some gentle spicing up is needed. This is achieved through a splash of pattern and a hint of extra colour. Here, the answer is a sumptuous embroidered brocade which elevates the Biedermeier sofa to glamorous new heights; while, for the stool, a tiny gingham in fresh lavender adds 'zip'.

**Above** Slinky satins, crisp cottons and lavish embroidery, all in understated shades of palest grey, lavender and ecru, create the basis for a sophisticated, salon style.

**Right** Extend a textural story through to the accessories. Where there is sheen on fabrics, look for equivalents in hard surfaces. Transluscent glass and shimmering silvery finishes are all complementary.

**Opposite** Formal rooms call for serious, elegant pieces of furniture. It is possible to draw together different styles by searching for thematic links. The boxy armchair and Gustavian console work in tandem, for example, because of their narrow, elegant legs; and even the panelled detail on the table is echoed in the silky stripe of the upholstery.

## Glamorous highlights

In a room planned as a grown-up retreat, mood is everything. A few well-chosen pieces of dark wood furniture will introduce grandeur, as will tailored upholstery, highlighted minimally with studding and self-piping. In general, sophistication is best maintained by an absence of frills, so the draped swags are kept crisp, and the slippery throw unadorned.

A chic, salon style like this also requires discipline when considering what is out on show. Piles of magazines and overstuffed bookshelves are anathema and should either be banished to another room or concealed behind storage that blends elegantly with the other furniture. Only then can decorative items be properly planned for display. Silver candlesticks and pewter echo the silvery grey palette; instead of pictures, etched wine glasses and mirrors play up the abundance of sunlight; and the vibrant fuchsia pink trace in the embroidered brocade is picked out in a vase full of hyacinths. Their heady perfume, combined with scented candles, provide an indulgent ambience just right for, say, an evening's entertaining.

**Opposite** In a dining room setting, look to china and table linen to echo decorative accenting that has already been established. Pearly bone handles, ornate silver detailing, crunchy quilted cloths and fine linen build on the translucence, sparkle and silvery colours already in place.

**Left** Fabric design can heavily influence the look of an upholstered piece. A stylized floral motif accentuates the curved, formal lines of the Biedermeier sofa.

**Above** A flawless and tailored room should have crisp window treatments. The sinuous drapes of swags are not only perfectly in keeping with the mood, but also show off the original window panelling. In a more relaxed room, a plain recessed blind or contrast colour on the panelling will suffice to dress the window while capitalizing on its glorious proportions.

# Colourful Collection

*A collection of beautiful objects, lovingly amassed over the years, can generate ideas that might define and direct the look of an entire room. This glorious collection of glass provides a wealth of inspiration for a room scheme. The exhilarating extremes of colour, the eccentric shapes and the mix of clear and opaque glass, encourage an experimental, artistic treatment for what was previously a plain country sitting room.*

**Above** A collection of glass vases is unified by a common theme, but it is often the idiosyncrasies, the clashes of texture and form, that provoke a more thoughtful interpretation.

**Right** Take an open-minded approach to architectural features, and do not let them dominate a design decision.

**Opposite** The plain fireplace in this rustic location did not have to mean a country cottage look. Rather its simplicity inspires a contemporary scheme in bold colours, and a confident mixture of classic and modern furniture styles.

The vivid shades of this glassware collection do not provide the basis for a colour scheme in the conventional sense. A combination of tangerine, jade, deep purple and turquoise, transposed literally onto walls and furniture, would be eccentric in the extreme. But this collection does provide the inspiration for using strong colours together, for playing with chance contrasts, just as they occur naturally within the collection. The impact of multicoloured glass vases ranged against an off-white wall can be recreated in a room using bold blocks of colour combined with more stable neutrals. Considered in this more abstract vein, colour can be used as a tool to define space.

This sitting room had little to recommend it architecturally; there was a low ceiling, a concrete floor and a very plain fireplace. The room also lacked atmosphere so colour is used to give the room a more quirky spirit.

**Left** Create a working sample-board in the room you are decorating. Start off with a notebook and fill it with experimental sketches, exploring the room from varying angles, adding paint chips, and small swatches of fabric. As you narrow down the choices, start to paint tiny sections of wall using sample pots, then pin up fabric favourites to check the effects of light on the different materials and the interplay of texture.

## A balancing act

For the colour scheme, four major shades are selected from the glassware: a vivid jade, a coppery blue-green, a canary yellow and deep purple. Before applying the colour, the space is turned into what amounts to a blank canvas: the walls are painted antique white and a floor is laid with pale oak woodblock. Next, each section of wall is painted either jade, blue-green or yellow, a treatment that both echoes the glassware and suggests a painterly environment. Each panel of colour is deliberately positioned next to an unassuming feature such as the fireplace or the alcove, which instantly injects character where none existed before. Finally, for a more textured effect, the wet paint is drybrushed, creating an impression of old plaster.

The bold panels of wall colour need to be balanced within the room with at least one other element in a similarly strong tone. Here, deep purple is used, which is incorporated into the scheme in the matt brushed cotton upholstery of the Art Deco furniture. The same fabric would have been too dark for the mahogany day bed, so pale green cotton with a seedling motif is used instead. This bridges the gap between bolds and neutrals seamlessly, and the pattern thematically hints at the garden just outside without detracting from the colour story within.

## Blocks and splashes

This scheme aims to surprise, so unusual accent colours and the way they are used are key elements. The juxtaposition of a bright turquoise tumbler next to an amethyst vase makes a striking contrast on the shelf; this contrast is daringly used as upholstery piping, too. The chartreuse of a handblown vase is reinterpreted as a scatter cushion, while the singing lime of another is painted as a panel on the wall. As the pinkish-mauve garden flowers in the vase look so good, scatter cushions and a bolster are made in the same colour.

**Left** When a collection has inspired an entire room, it is much more fun if it is given centre stage in the finished space. Coloured glass always looks spectacular on glass shelves, but if there is no suitable alcove, consider adding them to a recessed window. Taking pieces from the collection and placing them around the room makes everything much less formal. Some of the glassware in this collection is rearranged on the mantelpiece, and then filled with flowers for a less gallery-like feel.

# NATURAL LIGHT

*Simultaneously powerful and subtle, natural light awakens us, colours our feelings, and leaves us at the end of the day. We take it for granted, yet its gradual shift in depth and quality is constantly shaping our mood and the interiors we inhabit. The play of light can make a room tranquil and welcoming, dramatic or gloomy. Without it there would be none of the silhouettes, contrasts, or sunbeams that enhance the appeal of any interior. It affects the colours on our walls, our carefully chosen textures, and is the one natural element that must be taken into account when planning a room. Artists, photographers, interior designers and architects all try to capture it, but for everyone observation is the key. Watch what light does throughout the day (and seasons), and then exploit it to the full.*

## SOURCES OF INSPIRATION

We are all aware that naturally sunny rooms uplift us and gloomy ones do not. A sudden burst of sunshine warms and animates a room, the power of its light influencing a look and creating an ambience. And the fall and patterns of natural light can be explored and tapped into as a rich source of inspiration for decorating. Cool, diffuse light may suggest chalky, pale colours. Sun on square windowpanes might spark a chequerboard theme, while shady spaces might call for heavy textiles you are not usually drawn to. Let light guide you creatively, then work with it.

Locate the light source in your room and try to gauge its quality and intensity. Observe it at lunch- and teatime. Enjoy the sun setting, watch the shadows. Is it a morning or an evening room? Is the light right for its current function? Look at the way light comes through the windows. Does it create attractive shadows on a wall, are there powerful sunbeams that act as natural spotlights, or is the light always diffuse? If the room stays sombre even on a sunny day, does this bother you or might you capitalize on it? Do you find very strong sunlight distracting? Any of these things could be a starting point for the way you decorate. Pin down the mood created by the light and keep it in mind.

There are numerous ways of manipulating light within the home, and the effects can be striking. Observe it on a grand scale in historic houses or public buildings. Think of light streaming through mullioned windows and pooling on the floor, the cool tranquillity of a shady old church, the patterns of shadows cast from high windows in a library. Glance through art and photography books, focusing on light, shade and silhouettes, and observe how it can heighten colour to surreal depths, or to knock it dead. Look at interiors in magazines. Focus on the play of light in interiors of different styles. Mediterranean houses may suggest unusual ideas for coping with strong directional light; or use colours other than neutrals.

**Left** The addition of a skylight or conservatory-style roof is more structural, yet extremely effective in opening up a shady space. Plan your decoration to work with the direction of the light. The. creamy brown walls, stone floor and dark woods in this summer room look intensely dramatic cut through with slivers of sunlight.

**Right** Pale, creamy tones and a minimal amount of furniture in an attic bedroom make the most of little sunlight, as does a translucent sheer curtain caught back from an iron rod. A small or inset window requires special attention. Think about what is most appropriate, both to maximize light and to tie it in with the intended style of the room.

## USING LIGHT: BRIGHT ROOMS

Sun-filled rooms with ample windows are often the ones most used in the house. They generate a relaxed mood but encourage activity, and are ideal as kitchens, playrooms and living rooms. What does a surfeit of light suggest to you in terms of colours and textures? Do you want to exploit its sunny nature, or cool things down? Do you want to introduce an element of sophistication, or retain a casual feel? All light needs to be contained and directed, and your window treatments will significantly influence the style of a room.

For a sunny feel, look at colours that mimic and work with the sun's warm tones. This does not mean strong, bright colours; an excess of sunlight can fade and negate them. Think instead of the tones and shades that sunlight itself casts: soft tangerines, butter yellows, rosy pinks and the duskiest of reds. Even on cloudy days, such shades continue to suggest sunlight, and need only a hint of the real thing to bring a room to life. Consider, too, the impact of reflection. Wood or natural fibre floors in honey tones are more mellow than shiny

**Above** Even without strong sunlight, an all-white room is unfailingly bright. But such rooms need textures if they are to avoid a hint of chilliness in winter. Matt floorboards and woven cotton covers in white look and feel warm. Translucent blinds offer some control of light by directing and screening the rays. The flicker of a real fire is a welcome contrast on darker days.

**Opposite** Rather than attempting to compensate for the lack of light in a basement, use rich sombre colours to build on its intrinsic qualities and create a cosy atmosphere. This pale charcoal, taupe and white bedroom looks serene and inviting. Its modernist detailing draws attention away from the dearth of natural lighting. Fresh white bedlinen and paintwork suggest highlights where none actually exist.

whitewashed boards. Likewise, lean towards matt, textured fabrics that will absorb the sunlight – soft cottons, linens, and loose weaves rather than sheeny material. Small patterns have to work harder if there is a lot of light bouncing around. Try a large-scale design that will not be nearly as overpowering when light and shade are playing over walls or curtains.

The need to cool down a bright room calls not for deep, sombre shades, which might look dirty in the full glare of the sun, but for calming colours. Take a tip from hot countries where shady interiors are painted in tones of blue and green, from azure to midnight, seafoam to aqua. Stripes, whether on walls or upholstery, give an illusion of light and shade, and can cool things down visually. A dappled or distressed paint finish on the walls would suggest a play of shadows where they do not fall naturally.

Use light to influence mood and style naturally. To play up a sunny feel, choose curtain treatments that will diffuse the light. The most obvious, but classically simple, solution is to mix conventional lined curtains with roll-up blinds in the sheerest voile. You can take down the curtains in the height of summer and leave the blinds in place, or hang temporary summer 'curtains'. There are numerous floaty textiles available that can be simply sewn into hemmed rectangles and attached to an existing pole using curtain clips. Unlined Indian cottons in hot coloured stripes, simple florals, loose-weave linens and rough hessian (burlap) in neutral or deeper shades all look wonderful. Sheers have traditionally been available in white and neutrals, but now come in patterned designs, from floral to coloured checks, and look very pretty billowing in a gentle breeze. If you have deep-coloured walls, experiment with blinds made from sheer cotton in a colour to match the walls. Pulled down during the day, they will positively glow with colour.

The play of dark and light, slanting shadows and dramatic contrasts may have inspired your desire to cool down a room. Think about using roll-up blinds with blackout lining; classic, neutral blinds made from unbleached linen; or wooden Venetian blinds. Pull them halfway down to create dramatic slants of light or blocks of dark and shade across walls and floor. In Georgian or Victorian houses with sash windows, consider the possibility of reinstating authentic internal, wooden shutters that fold fully or partly across the panes. Shutters are brilliant for engineering pools of light and shade, and often look best without curtains. For more organic light patterns, consider growing a creeper around a window so that it throws pretty shadows on the wall as the sun swings around. You could allow it to cover a large part of a bathroom window as a natural screen, and an odd tendril escaping inside will look charming.

Not all bright rooms will benefit from direct sunlight. Some have a colder, more diffuse northern light; or light may filter through frosted glass panes installed to provide privacy or conceal an unpleasant view. This bright but restrained light brings opportunities for playing with softer, more subtle shades. Where harsh yellow sunshine might have bleached them to obscurity, ice blues, greys and lichen green can take on a restful tranquillity when used in bright cool light. Use them in layers of differing tones, for walls, floors and upholstery; the all-over wash of colour will give an illusion of soft, constant light. Add touches of off-white to suggest gentle highlights if they are naturally lacking. An all-white room could look spectacular, but keep shapes and textures soft and welcoming to avoid any hint of clinical unfriendliness. Shadow play in a neutral room can be particularly fascinating; think of the varying tones of a sepia photo as you experiment.

## USING LIGHT : DARKER ROOMS

Suggest painting a dark room in inky blue or mushroom, and most people think you are mad. But if you are faced with one or a series of gloomy spaces, perhaps a narrow hall and staircase, a back bedroom or a basement, it can make sense to accept and work with the sombre tones. Look at a seventeenth-century Dutch interior painting with its pools of light, deep colours and contrast chequerboard floors, and you will see there is grandeur in dark rooms.

If you accept that your space does not have a sunny ambience, you can enjoy choosing colours to promote serenity or create a cosy element of retreat: earthy neutrals, sand, stone, dappled shades of forest green; or deep sea turquoise and aqua for an underwatery feel. Flat, matt walls will probably work better than busy wallpaper, and look good with a textured and patterned rug. For contrast and highlights choose a creamy neutral rather than stark white. Use blocks around the room – in picture frames, scatter cushions, an armchair, or a lavish throw. To take things darker, introduce heavy wood furniture; or tread a mid-line using blond wood or colourwashed pieces. In such a scheme, windows and the amount of light they allow through become less important. Add to the rich ambience by hanging simple but heavily textured curtains in a tone to match the walls.

On balance, you may want to make your room as light as possible and this could lead you back to softer, paler shades. Surfaces that impart a subtle sheen, reflect or bounce light, or let it stream through, will all help to create a more vibrant environment. Glass-topped and plastic furniture, gloss paint, large mirrors, rakish chandeliers, or even mirror balls for the trendy, will all capture rays of light.

Go for pale-coloured blinds that still provide an effective screen at night, or those with punched holes that allow sunshine through. Use flat voile screens to filter light yet provide privacy from the street. Keep essential curtains pale and unlined. Cream and off-white linen or canvas can suggest sun where there is none. Similarly, keep flooring as light as possible. Consider bleached or whitewashed floorboards; pale, grey-toned linoleum; or pastel chequerboards.

However you choose to use natural light, make major changes before you decorate. What about a wall of glass bricks; stainless-steel in a kitchen or a modern interior; or fewer internal doors? Sandblasted or etched glass obviate the need for light-restricting curtains.

### MAKING IT HAPPEN

If quality of light is your starting point, it will lead logically to colour and fabric. Consider the physical effects of colours and patterns and observe them at varying times imagining how light may alter them through the seasons.

The position of furniture also affects the play of light. A sparsely furnished room, with plenty of space around pieces, gives a fresh feel. Think about materials, not only light-refracting ones like plastic and glass, but also slim-legged cane furniture, wrought-iron garden chairs, or glistening chrome and aluminium. Look at translucent materials, from blow-up plastic armchairs to the colourful polypropylene favoured by modern designers. Heavy, dense but comfortable furniture helps to create a richly warm and intimate interior, and can be placed so as to produce deep shadows or strong silhouettes.

Whatever window treatment you settle on, you will need to hang voiles, unlined fabrics and blind textiles up at the light source, watching for differences when the fabric is gathered or spread flat. An experienced blind-maker will know if it is feasible to use a particular sheer for a blind, and whether or not it needs lining. Search out other specialists for custom-made shutters, glass bricks, etched glass and the shiniest of surfaces.

**Opposite** Natural light defines window shapes and what is beyond, as well as effecting gradations of light and dark within a room. This picture window is left undressed to focus attention on a wonderful vista. It frames a porch lamp, a bird sculpture and a lush garden. Stone-coloured paint highlights the window frame, giving it a strong connection to the modern art gracing the walls.

**Above** A family sitting room where adults and children gather informally needs to feel friendly and inviting. If it lacks sunbeams, suggest them with warm tones. The dusky salmon pinks on the walls and touches of corn yellow in the unlined blinds make this room vital and welcoming. White covers, a pale floor and distressed wooden furniture reflect and bounce around the available sunlight.

**Below** Translucent glass, pure, clean shapes and pale, bleached tones create the illusion of natural sunshine, even if it is in short supply.

**Right** A summery, rose-sprigged bedroom is guaranteed to lift the spirits. Yellow is a cheerful and calming colour, and layering tone on tone from dense cream to sharp lemon produces a fresh, yet relaxing effect.

**Opposite** A splash of brilliant, natural sunlight gives any room an acute natural advantage.

# Radiant Spaces

*A blast of sunlight in a big, square room is a tantalizing beginning for a decorating scheme. But if you cast a glance beyond the window, you can use the view to source inspirational images that you can then employ inside. This country bedroom overlooks a beautiful flower garden and beyond that fields, making the view a visual feast in the summer. Butter yellows with fresh white, a dash of pure pink, and the curls of opening rosebuds form a natural, irresistible starting point.*

Above all, a bedroom needs to be comfortable, but it also needs an intimate atmosphere. It should be a stimulating place to start the day, and a cosy retreat for shutting out the world. If you control the light filtering in, the mood will naturally follow. Awash with sunlight, this room could feel cold because big windows and broad proportions can make a room seem cavernous. Glowing, friendly colours are needed to enhance the sunshine, and individual focuses need to be created within the room to break up the large space: an area for sleeping, one for relaxing and one for dressing.

A bedroom also needs personality along with a sense of style. Rejecting the received country house or rustic cottage image, the owners wanted something pretty with a

breezy atmosphere. Classic roses from the garden set the scene. Timelessly appealing, they can be as contemporary or retrospective as you wish and, mixed with plain, fresh colours, will create a chic, modern look.

## *The perfect yellow*

Yellow is a notoriously difficult shade to get right, but, once achieved, it is one of the easiest and most glorious colours to live with. It is never out of fashion and is always welcoming, whatever the weather outside. Yet finding that perfect shade can be a struggle. Too much green and it will look sharp, too creamy and it will be insipid, too strong and you will be living with custard. Experimentation is the key, especially in a sunny room. Sunlight tends to bleach out yellows that look strong on paint swatches so paint small patches in different tones on the walls of an empty room and observe the effects over the course of a week.

Where contrasting colours might create a conflict of attention, a combination of yellows, from creamy linen tones to buttercup and lemon, works with the sun to create a flood of colour throughout the room. Use translucent textiles and pale surfaces to enhance the light. Poor floorboards can be painted white, but remember that in a bedroom comfort is paramount. Here, a sisal-wool mix ivory carpet reflects light upwards and is soft underfoot. Natural weaves are no longer restricted to neutral shades, but are available in a wide spectrum of colours.

Big windows need to be considered carefully so that the flow of light can be controlled. These windows have their original panelling and shutters intact, but what may look elegantly unadorned in a drawing room will look positively bare in a bedroom. Dress curtains give a more delicate finish, while shutters can be used to screen very bright sunlight and can be closed at night for privacy. Choose a fabric that looks its best unlined: here a loose-weave cream linen gently filters the sun and moves in the breeze of an open window. Plain fabrics are more practical because gentle colour and pattern is easily bleached out by the sun.

**Left** A single fabric design can be used in several guises throughout a room. A classic, rose-print cotton becomes an oilcloth for a kitchen chair seat, seamlessly blending furniture and bedlinen. Look, too, for designs reinterpreted on filmy voiles which are perfect for dress curtains in light, bright rooms.

**Opposite** The open weaves of voile and linen, in single tones, with accents of white, are essential components for a light-enhancing scheme.

**Above** Little bedroom luxuries – a soft, padded hanger, hand-embroidered linens for mixing and matching, and a spare quilt for chilly nights – add extra nuances of colour to the scheme.

105

Around the four-poster bed voile dress curtains are also filmy and unlined, yet their yellow-and-white stripes show up clearly away from the light source.

## A rose-sprigged bed

In a bedroom of plain fabrics, the bed can afford to be indulgently patterned. Just for a change, eschew monastic white bedlinen and switch the focus to decadent blossom-strewn designs. A rose-sprigged duvet with dashes of pink and a scattering of white dots sets the tone for a pure and pretty style, and adds all the extra colour required as a foil for the buttercup yellows. Look out for bedlinens which can be bought with matching fabric. Scatter cushions in the same print draw together the bed and sofa area, and a matching oilcloth brightens up an old kitchen chair. Conversely, remember that bedding can be custom-made; you do not have to rely on ready-made designs. Thick quilted cottons, like this plaid, can be stitched into wonderful bedcovers. This, too, is echoed in the scatter cushion on the sofa. The goal in a bedroom is to create a bed that looks inviting. Good-quality pillows, a plump duvet (comforter) and a firm mattress are indispensable.

## Pure country style

Furniture choices maintain the simple and fresh country style. Unremarkable pieces — a cumbersome armoire, an old kitchen chair, a 1950s-style side table, and a long, narrow sofa — are solid and unassuming, neither too rustic nor too ornate. Reinvented with a wash of white emulsion (latex) and, for the sofa, a loose slipcover in a sheer lemon linen, they are chic in style and provide the perfect contrast to the prettiness of the bed.

**Above** A twirly wrought-iron bedstead and feather-light dress curtains ensure a sunny, airy feel.

**Right** A pure and simple style needs the odd glamorous fillip. The beaded pendant adds a sophisticated touch to an otherwise utilitarian armoire, while other light-refracting details, like a crystal droplet hanging from a light pull and a glass bead-encrusted doorknob, add sparkle, too.

**Opposite** An intimate seating area, with a sofa for lounging on and a side table for easy breakfasts, fills up the vast floor space.

# SPACE

*Space to stride through, stretch out in, chase the kids, or party; corners to snuggle in; vistas from room to room. We all have a natural desire for space in our homes, yet this precious commodity is disappearing fast. Modern homes are frequently small, and grander houses are divided up into apartments. In search of larger living spaces, city dwellers are exploring lofts, converted factories, schools and dockside warehouses. Each presents a unique dilemma. Too little space and we feel claustrophobic; too much and we take fright, fearing a loss of intimacy. With money, time and commitment you can surely move walls, build up and out, add and take away. But if these are not available to you, artful planning with what you have and skilful illusion can also work wonders.*

**Left** The glory of an open-plan loft is the absence of restrictive internal walls. Yet, even the most free-spirited of living quarters needs some way to distinguish areas for different functions such as eating, sleeping, entertaining and working. It is often better to use colour and form than to erect physical partitions. Here, a background of pure white walls and bleached wooden floorboards emphasizes the feeling of space. Skinny blocks of cool navy kitchen cupboards and a contemporary rug define key areas, without overpowering the seamless expanse of the whole.

**Opposite** In a small studio apartment, a block of solid colour on a wall marks out a sleeping area from the rest of the space. Your choice of colour is as important as how you use it. A sombre navy blue creates a feeling of peace.

## SOURCES OF INSPIRATION

The way we live today requires us to re-evaluate our living spaces. We may have extended families, work at home, and prefer flexible, less formal environments.

Generous, meagre or plain irregular, a room's proportions exert a fundamental influence. We should not overlook them in the exciting search for pretty fabrics or paint colours. Stand in an empty room considering the needs created by its proportions, and decorating ideas will come to you. Your creative thoughts may not stir until faced with a practical problem. A low-ceilinged, poky spare room or a draughty drawing room can open your mind to new ideas. An outsize, flower-strewn wallpaper design rejected for the bedroom might be used to distract attention from a difficult space. Replacing two shabby sofas with one huge one will change the spatial proportions of a room.

Make yourself aware of how others use space. Chic, large-scale restaurants, clothes shops, or interior-designed hotels may suggest ideas for lighting, furniture placement or flower arrangements in bigger spaces, or clever ways to link one room to another. Take photographs; amass pictures from magazines; look at the proportions of furniture; and adapt ideas about storage, which is vital, whatever size of space you have.

## USING SPACE : LARGE ROOMS

A big living space is exhilarating. You get all the benefits of a high ceiling, large windows and space, even if the one room has to accommodate a variety of activities. If it is a room with a single function, so much the better. Huge rooms give lots of scope for interpretation. You can go for a grand style if architectural detailing allows; experiment with minimalism; show off furniture; display large pieces of art. Decoratively, you can be experimental because unusual patterns or colours will not be in such sharp focus. Yet, great expanses can be cold and draughty; dwarf existing furniture; diminish a carefully chosen pattern; and be very expensive to decorate.

If you want to make the room more intimate, and you like the effects of pattern, strong designs will generally lessen the feeling of space. Tall walls and expansive furniture can take the drama of big, bold stripes, trailing floral bouquets, flying birds, of space, then work to enhance it. Matt-painted walls in white or cool, bright colours, the reflective surfaces of stainless steel or zinc, an expanse of pale marble or bleached oak floor, will all result in a greater feeling of space. Emphasize the height of tall windows with slim, unlined curtain panels on a narrow, high pole, or roll-up blinds that retract out of sight during the day.

Big rooms demand bold furniture, so consider selling or swapping key pieces to get the scale right. If that is not an option, consider how to place smaller pieces. Grouping sofas and chairs around one or two coffee tables in the centre of the room allows for intimacy, whilst maintaining a feeling of spaciousness. Plumb a large-scale bath in the middle of a bathroom; or even in a big bedroom, and make the connecting bath-room into a dressing room. If it is modern minimalism you are after, have very little furniture, so long as it is quirky or unusual enough to merit the attention it will attract. A few major accessories – a giant gilded mirror, a single large vase with flowers on a grand scale, an outsize standard lamp – will have a greater impact than a host of smaller objects.

## USING SPACE: SMALL ROOMS

A room may feel cramped because it was built that way or because it is in a converted property. Smaller spaces have their merits, though; they can be cosy retreats and are easy to keep warm. Moreover, it may be the one room in the house that is your own. They can also be frustratingly difficult to furnish, with a narrow door that excludes furniture, or only enough floor space for a sofabed. Storage potential will be limited, light may be poor because of small windows, or the proportions

or modern geometrics. The bigger the repeat pattern, the better. Take care to avoid too regular a motif, which on a large scale may realign into irritating diagonals, particularly on wallpaper. But archive designs, originally destined for large houses, may have a more irregular distribution across a large expanse. Unless you want to create a textural effect, steer clear of smaller patterns. Layer patterns in varying scales and designs, not only for a visual feast but also because they will give the illusion of intimacy. Heavily textured curtains, broad pelmets (valances) and lambrequins, chunky curtain poles and the use of pattern will bring down the height of large windows.

The judicious use of strong, bright or warm colours will reduce a cavernous feel. If, on the other hand, you have bought your loft apartment specifically because you love the feeling

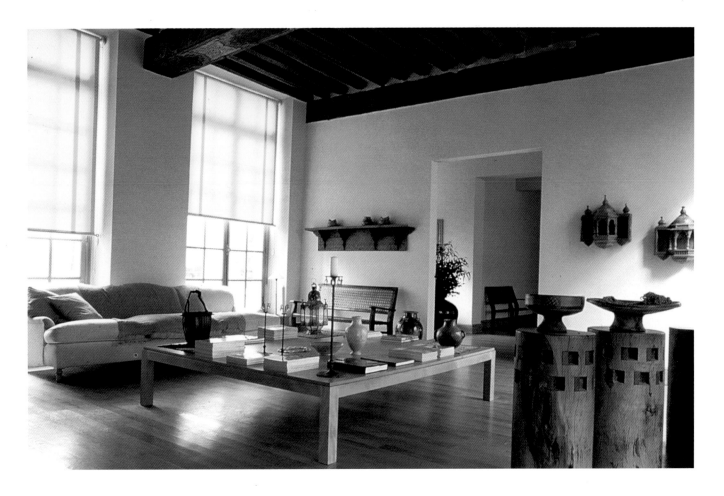

may be odd. Reduce frustration by thinking how a room is to be used. If a kitchen is big enough to include a dining area, it is far better to reinvent the dining room as a study than to struggle with furniture that simply will not fit.

Turn problems to your advantage. Lots of detail in a small room can distract the eye from tiny proportions and trick it into thinking everything is much grander. You can indulge in small-scale prints, weaves and needlepoint fabrics because they will be seen up close and be on smaller pieces of furniture. Texture, too, takes on fresh significance. Try tactile wool, suede or brushed cotton on chairs or curtains, with cushions and throws in something silkier for contrast. If the room is to be a retreat, choose deep, warm colours to enhance the mood and cram in lots of pictures, books and favourite things.

**Opposite** A vast wall mirror never fails visually to push back the walls of a small room. The illusion of space is further enhanced by using a subtle monochrome palette, simple block shapes, and minimal accessories.

**Above** Decorating an enormous room requires careful planning and furniture that is in proportion. Small furniture would look insignificant. Such a room needs stretched sofas, outsize tables and massive cupboards. The towering windows in this continental sitting room are brought down to human scale by half-lowering the blinds. Similarly, artefacts are hung midway up the wall.

If you need to push back the walls visually in a main living space, choose colours in pale, matt shades; ruthlessly cut down on furniture; and keep accessories to a minimum. Try tricks, vertically striped walls, say, to make the ceiling seem higher; or remove central pendant light fittings; and keep floors pale and reflective. Floor-to-ceiling cupboards with unadorned doors, painted to blend in with the walls, form the least obtrusive storage solution. Use alcoves or the space above a door for cupboards or shelves. And keep the floor space as empty as possible. Trim beds and sofas with long skirts to conceal storage space.

## LINKING SPACES

Every house has its own configuration of linking spaces that offer an extra decorating dimension. When planning a new scheme, consider the colours of your hallway and staircase or, even better, change them too. Play with unity or unexpected contrasts. Choose a main fabric colour from the sitting room and use it in the hall to unify the two spaces. Or use one of your accent colours in the hall for a surprising yet cohesive contrast. Have a fresh look at co-ordinated fabric collections that include stripes and checks with a large- and smaller-scale main pattern. Use one combination in the principal room, and another in the adjoining room to create a subtle change of tone.

The view from one room to the next is invariably framed by a doorway. You might remove the door and paint the architrave a different colour to highlight the frame. Exploit the area beyond to create a deliberate tableau with a curvy item of furniture, a favourite picture, or a display of flowers.

## DEFINING SPACE

Large kitchens that have enough space for eating, working and socializing, are today often the heart of a house and take precedence over formal sitting rooms. The blurring of physical

**Left** A pitched ceiling, out-of-kilter walls, or any unusually proportioned space requires extra thought. A sloping roof beam could have dominated this small room. Instead, it is a characterful feature in a dining area where ceiling height is not so vital.

**Below** In a modern kitchen where light is essential and through traffic inevitable, a light-refracting screen supported on elegant struts is ideal to define the work space. Planned with an eye for proportion and detail, a screen is a thing of beauty, too.

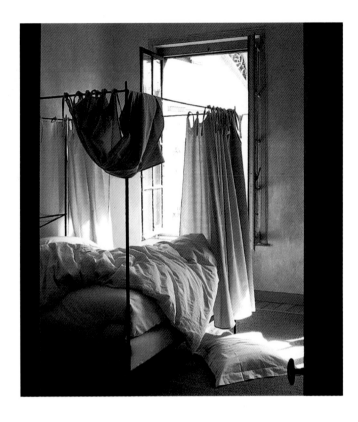

**Left** A substantial piece of furniture can work in a small room if the space surrounding it remains uncluttered. Four-poster beds are most often found in grand interiors, but this light and elegant design looks intimate and inviting in a room where the yellow ochre walls have been left deliberately unadorned. The filmy bed drapes diffuse and soften the light as it passes through.

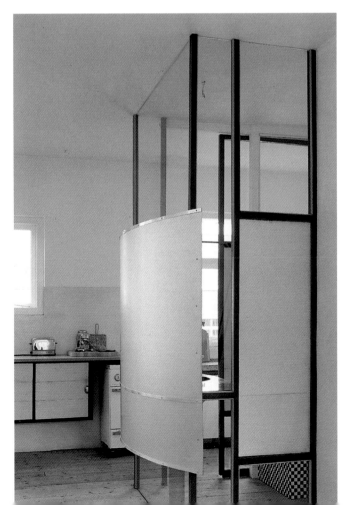

boundaries within a home means that more people live, work and play within single, larger spaces. You may want to consider ways of defining open-plan areas, so that everyone is clear where they can be busy and where they should be calm. You could use different colours to designate spatial boundaries, for example. Create an abstract pattern as a decorative dividing line across a floor. Or the sunny side of an apartment might be devoted to areas of daytime activity; and the darker side reserved for after-dark entertaining, bathing (plumbing permitting), and sleeping.

If you prefer or need physical divisions, install large wooden dividing doors across a sitting room to create a social space and a work or play area. Or run a curtain pole across at ceiling height. Experiment with roll-up blinds as partitions. Contemporary spaces might call for sliding doors, or large screens on wheels. With these physical boundaries, you may want to keep the adjoining spaces in style.

# Minimal Dimensions

*Strictures on space necessitate inventive solutions. Small and dark, with the worst of views, a tiny room reinvents itself in a fresh new guise. In the scramble for space, a home office can be created out of the humblest of dimensions, and yet it can still offer imaginative surprises. Lack of space calls for restraint, organization and punctilious order. Here, the soothing colours of indigo and taupe, sourced from balls of string, provide the parameters for an oasis of calm.*

A small store room presents myriad problems. Dimensions may seem hopelessly unworkable, light may be scanty, and the atmosphere may be non-existent. Empty and unloved, and measuring just 2 x 2.5m (2¼ x 2¾yd), this tiny

room looked so small that the thought of furnishing it seemed daunting. The room is also north-facing, with gloomy shadows and a cool air. However, it still has potential. A tape measure, run along the walls and around potential furniture, establishes that there is room for basics – so long as you apply a little judicious forethought. The generous sash window provides the focus of one wall, and supplies plenty of light for a study area. At the same time, that diffuse and shady light prompts a rethink in mood. After all, a study needs to be soothing and composed. Teamed with underwater colours and gently glinting surfaces, shady light can be turned to an advantage, generating a studious atmosphere and a crisp and workmanlike style.

**Above** The oatmeal hues of string, the creamy beige of a manilla envelope or the pastel colours of a postage stamp can all provide a multitude of colour inspirations.

**Left** The luxury of having a separate home office makes the tiniest of rooms look appealing.

**Opposite** Rigorous planning of equipment is vital in a home office: the computer terminal, printer, fax, telephone and answer machine all need to be accessible, with wires and cables tucked well out of the way.

## Small-scale planning

A sliver of workable space is only as useful as its capacity for storage, which needs to be planned with rigorous precision. In a home office, more than any other room, efficiency is paramount. The basics – a desk, a back-supporting chair, storage for papers and other paraphernalia – need to be sorted out first. Then, if there is any remaining space, you can think about introducing additions such as an arm-chair for relaxed reading. Think practically about cupboards. There might not be enough room to open and close doors, making open-faced shelving preferable. In order to take up minimal floor space, stack storage into a tall, narrow structure. In this room, conventional office equipment is jettisoned in favour of more unusual pieces: a Gustavian-style table doubles as a desk and a slim, galvanized-steel drawer unit holds the bulk of home office filing.

The shape, finish and placement of furniture in a room will inevitably have an impact on the space. Be aware of this and look for themes to highlight. The almond-coloured wood and silvery steel of the desk and drawer unit create an

**Above**  Rules are relaxed in a home office. A radio for catching the lunchtime news, flowers on the desk and the indulgence of ink instead of ballpoint pens are enticing extras.

**Right**  An understated mix of plain linens and a business-like ticking make for a calming, tailored scheme centred around blues and neutrals. Investing time to decorate a home office properly pays dividends: it feels like a proper work space and makes it a pleasurable place to be.

**Opposite**  Even the smallest of spaces can be stretched to accommodate a working area and a relaxing corner. Counteract the harsh angles of technology with a curvy chair, a floppy cushion and an unstructured laundry bag for magazines and books. A picture on the wall in place of calendars and clocks promotes a cosier ambience.

**Right** Utilize spare wall space for individual storage boxes, so that pencils, postcards, notepads and string are easily at hand.

**Below** The ubiquitous office pinboard gets a revamp. A silvery memo board is practical, yet when stuck with favourite art postcards it looks beautiful, too.

Window treatments in small rooms are just as important as those in larger ones. In an office, some form of screen is essential, especially if a workstation is to be situated near direct sunlight, which may need to be blocked out. However, curtains take up precious wall space and reduce the amount of light in dark rooms. A blind, conversely, can be rolled up out of the way. Instead of the more utilitarian roll-up blind, a Roman blind has been chosen as its pleated folds and contrast edging soften the hard angles of office equipment, creating a gentler environment. A vertical crisp ticking stripe is used to create the illusion of height. With a touch of irony, its shirty stripes are a visual reference to the conventions of an office world left far behind.

initial visual tension between grainy and shiny surfaces; on a broader plane, this can be seen as a juxtaposition between antique lines and contemporary styling, which sets a pattern for the rest of the room. The blond-wood shelf unit contrasts with the creamy brushstrokes on the traditional drawer chest; tubular steel and pale ply meet in the swivel chair; and accessories also take up the theme.

## A tranquil palette

A tiny space will need to be extended visually: the ceiling needs to be pushed up, and the walls forced back. Colours and patterns can be either beneficial or intrusive, so they need to be chosen with care. In its new role as a home office, this small room also needs a calm, soothing palette. Blue is a natural choice for a working environment; it is associated with restful thought and, provided the right shade is chosen, it is cooling rather than cold. A true, ocean aqua – opt for paint rather than fussier wallpaper – revitalizes the dull walls, and provides a plain, serene backdrop to counteract the inevitable clutter of office equipment and stationery. Crisp white paintwork emphasizes the window, and ensures that it remains a central feature in the room.

**Left** Plan storage within storage. An open shelf unit in a tiny room calls for neat, orderly lines. A substantial number of small boxes, files and tins keep papers, reference material, stationery and disks in check. Mix and match contrasting styles to spruce up the look of a plain shelf: navy linen and rose-patterned wallpaper, aluminium with mock croc, and punched tin with acrylic. All these styles blend together within the confines of a silver, neutral and blue palette.

Restricted space works better with a restricted palette, and fabric choices should reflect the tones already established in a room scheme. Here a cosy armchair smartens up in neutral linen, and a hyacinth blue fabric graces the office chair. No-nonsense sisal matting on the floor is similarly neutral, maximizing the available floor space.

## Classic meets contemporary

A principal delight of the home office is that it can be full of the latest technology, and yet it still remains infinitely more welcoming than an office at work. Office chairs can be covered in linen and storage boxes in flower-strewn wallpaper.

Accessorizing becomes much more fun when everyday objects – a raffia basket, a fabric laundry bag – can be turned into storage facilities, and when the luxury of comfort raises the tone.

The accessories in this office take up the classic and contemporary themes: a retro silver lamp hovers over a state-of-the-art computer terminal; metal tea tins and linen-covered disk files contrast with acrylic and chrome boxes; the pinboard is hi-tech chrome, while the pictures are framed art photographs. Together, they provide a visual feast. Yet, essential to small-space living, these same items are carefully arranged on the shelves to promote unity of line, and the illusion of order. In tiny rooms, the visual tricks really do count.

# ARCHITECTURAL DETAIL

*Sometimes grand, often rather modest, there are some rooms that positively shout for attention. They are so beautifully constructed that they simply cannot be ignored. A generous ceiling moulding, lofty floor-to-ceiling sash windows or glazed doors, a gently curved wall or arched doorway, or an intricately tiled fireplace; all such features capture our gaze and please our senses. Period architecture is crammed with special details; you may not love them all but any sensitive decorator will work with and around them. You may admire windows for their symmetry, and cornicing for its intricacy. Or enjoy the way time has worn and moulded floors, bent door frames, cracked and characterized original plaster walls. But re-evaluate, too, what features modern buildings have to offer.*

**Above** Modern features in a classically proportioned room can look beautiful as well as radical. Here, the gentle scroll of ironwork on the balcony and the ornate cornice detailing are appreciated afresh when seen in contrast to the clean-cut lines of a modern fireplace and contemporary furniture. A white palette unifies the period and modern styles.

**Opposite** Whether a house is grand or humble, cultivate the art of faking architectural detail where none exists. Many houses lack character because original features have been removed or were in short supply at the time of building. A confident strip of navy at the base of saffron yellow walls gives definition to this cottage interior. Consider how to make the most of vistas framed by open doors.

## SOURCES OF INSPIRATION

Most of us recognize the importance of preserving original architectural features, but, after the craze for Victoriana, modernism again beckons. Rather than seek to restore authentically, we tend to use individual period features to inspire and direct us. Mosaic floor tiles in a grand old house may suggest a modern use of sombre, chalky shades; or sash windows with original shutters may become part of a contemporary, less-is-more interior. So, scour your interior for architectural details that might inspire a fresh idea. But do not look at a room in isolation because detailing is likely to recur in slight variations throughout the house.

Consider the proportions and major features of a room: the doors, windows, floor and fireplace. Windows dominate, so their style is likely to set a decorative tone. Look at textures and shades. Do dark floorboards inspire a play of chocolate and cream neutrals? A grey marble fireplace might suggest a combination of cool surfaces. Is there a a plaster frieze, a fireplace tile: what motifs do they contain? An abstract swirl, or some tiny birds or roses could set off a theme. If intricate plasterwork has lost its definition under many layers of paint, work back to the original.

If inspiration lies in the physical shape and presence of one feature, most likely a dramatic fireplace or unusually shaped window, devise a scheme to throw attention onto it. If rooms lack detail, search through catalogues of fireplaces, mouldings and tiles, and books on architectural detailing and the history of interior design. Visit architectural salvage yards and poke about in builders' rubble; you never know what you might find. But if blue-and-white Delft tiles inspire you to impose a complete Dutch parlour period look, exercise a little restraint. A looser interpretation might be less time-consuming and more creative.

## USING EXISTING FEATURES

In a house blessed with original features, such as wall panelling or slim Georgian windows with inset seats and wooden shutters, it is tempting to decorate in period style with authentic paint colours and finishes, appropriate furniture, and archive fabric designs. But remember your home is not a museum; it is somewhere for you to live and enjoy. Attempt such a recreation with humour and a light touch so that you interpret a period feel and capture a mood. Certain architectural features call not for a

period interpretation but, rather, for a general empathy. An old house or country cottage with wide, worn floorboards and bumpy plaster can cry out for traditional paints in dusky shades. But modern upholstery and curtain treatments in crisp utility fabrics would look more upbeat than the customary florals and patchwork quilts.

Treat elegant period details such as parquet floors, tall windows or grand fireplaces as simply as possible, rather than detract from them with fussy curtains or very grand mirrors. Mix them with contemporary pieces of furniture or brightly coloured walls. Such unexpected combinations create drama, surprise, and a new focus. Or try setting a period sofa against the whitewashed brick wall of a converted warehouse.

If a floor tile or perhaps a stained-glass window has a significant design or motif, adapt it to create a room scheme. An organic design, a leaf or an apple, could be echoed in patterned textiles – or on other hard surfaces in the room. You may want a new radiator cover made of fibreboard. Trace the original motif, photocopy it up to the right proportions and have it cut out of the cover. Bold-scale stencilling still has a place in some decorative schemes, so use your pattern to hand-cut a stencil. If your inspiration stems from a more abstract pattern, such as a carved trellis design, consider repeating it as a painted or stencilled design on the floor, as part of a built-in shelf detail, or sandblasted onto glass.

Architectural features can act as decorative *objets d'art*. A weathered arched window frame could simply be propped against a wall or secured above a fireplace, or a piece of detailed moulding hung as a picture. Similar finds would be fun seen emerging from a cluster of leafy indoor plants.

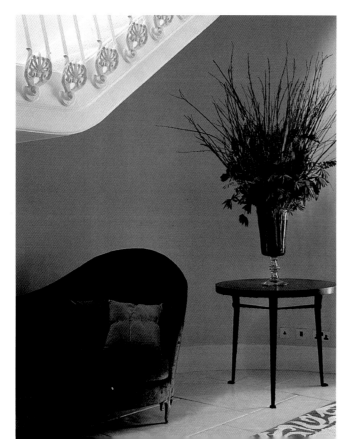

## ADDING FEATURES

Architectural features shape and define a room; without them a space may appear bare and impersonal. They can be added, whether it is moulded plasterwork or a different kind of door, or faked. Although making changes stylistically can create wonderful surprises, a room with a mix of grand Swedish Gustavian panelling and enormous Victorian radiators might look rather odd. Visit houses similar to yours; you may find one that still has original features that could guide you. And do not forget to balance scale.

If doors and windows have been replaced with modern aluminium frames, or they lack panelling, a primary concern will be to revert to original styles. It is better to spend money on getting the bare bones right, and choose a less expensive decorating scheme. And classic, chunky, central heating radiators do look much nicer than trim modern ones. Authentic is not always best, however. In a cool, contemporary sitting room it might be better visually to swap an original heavy black fireplace for a curvier marble French-style one, despite a cross-over of styles. If you add detailed cornices for grandeur, it does not mean you have to have dado rails, too.

As decorating looks are simpler nowadays, add details only to create definition rather than as extraneous clutter. Too many modern or converted properties are given thin, meagre-looking skirting boards (baseboards), whereas a generous 23cm (10in) board with a complex moulding adds enriching detail and a solid base to a room. To change the look of a room radically, consider full or partial panelling created by a specialist carpenter, or ready-made panelling designed to slot together.

So that added features do not look new or fake, blend them in by using as many original materials as possible. Have a carpenter rework beautiful, discarded wood panelling as an architrave. When the real thing is not available, try visual tricks. Paint new wooden shutters or skirtings (baseboards) and gently distress them to match a painted antique in the room. Highlight and slightly age mouldings by adding a faint line of a darker shade of paint, or a subtle hint of broken gilding. Mouldings look more authentic if they are painted in a mix of muted neutrals rather than pristine white.

Architectural definition can be hinted at with paint, if it is used cleverly. A bold line of colour can trick the eye. If there is no moulding but the ceiling is high, consider painting the ceiling in a deep shade, taking the colour down as far as an imaginary cornice. Likewise, a painted strip at the base of a wall will suggest a skirting (base) board. Broad strips of colour around windows and doors without architraves will help to define them. Or coloured tiles could be used in place of the painted strip. Although you need a lot of confidence to create

**Opposite** Decorative ironwork can be a rich source of inspiration. The intricately curved bases of this period balustrade have become a design template. It is not slavishly copied, but subtly interpreted in the hall below it: in a loose swirl on the border of the carpet, in the organic curve of a velvety chaise longue, and in the curvaceous legs of the table.

**Above** This mad mix of different architectural styles gathered together in one room might have been a disaster. The ornate mantel, solidly simple fireplace, and tongue-and-groove wall panelling in this informal sitting room hail from very different eras. But when they are all painted white, one's attention is directed, instead, to the family's favourite treasures – an oil painting, an antique textile, a child's chair.

*127*

glazed cupboards. Imagine a soft tangerine backdrop to blue-and-white china, or grey behind cranberry-coloured glasses.

## THE PRACTICALITIES

As a purist, you will want to restore precious details, stick to authentic materials, and hover around the historically correct boundaries. But the cost of restoring a feature may far outweigh the price of replacing it with something almost identical; and the use of an authentic paint finish may not be practical for late twentieth-century living. Putting in an authentic plaster moulding may give you pleasure, but once it is painted, it will look much the same as a cheaper resin one. But beware. Some are clumsily drawn, so scrutinize cheaper resin or wood mouldings and detailing for their quality of design. They will often look cheap no matter how you paint them. The same goes for reproduction fireplaces. Prices vary enormously between styles but choose the best one you can afford as it will be a major focal point.

false panelling on walls, perhaps by copying a pattern from a book of historical interiors, the results can be utterly convincing, as can painting fake tiles onto floors or walls.

Traditionally, white or a pale neutral is used for ceilings and woodwork, but it is fun to use colour for mouldings, around doors, or on wooden floors. It does not have to be a strongly contrasting colour, simply a slightly paler shade of that on the walls, or one of the colours in the wallpaper. Using colour like this highlights lovely architectural detailing; adds emphasis if the architraves are not spectacular; and lends confidence and cohesion to a decorative scheme. To draw instant attention to displays, try painting the interiors of built-in shelves or

Armed with your design, and having decided how you are going to put it all together, and the quality you are hoping to achieve, the last stage, as always, is to find specialist suppliers. Look at catalogues to consider both cheap options and companies specializing in faithful period copies, traditional materials and modern versions. Search out architectural salvage yards and, importantly, a creative carpenter to adapt your finds sympathetically. Gather historically correct paint charts and discuss your needs with paint specialists. They are a mine of information and most are quite used to mixing a special colour to match the minutest chip of original paint.

**Opposite** Updated cream panelling and simple styling in this bedroom successfully combine modernity with respect for the original features.

**Left** Have no qualms about faking architectural features. Panelling is one of the easiest effects to try. Ready-made mouldings are simply glued to the wall, and when painted look just as elegant as the real thing.

**Above** The bold rectangular shapes of the contemporary furniture blend easily with the simple geometric design of the panelling in this period interior. Just as easily, the herringbone patterns of the polished wood floor might have inspired the use of textiles with related textures or patterns.

*129*

# A Dominant Fireplace

*A fireplace is a centralizing feature. By day, it forms a natural decorative focus, dominating a room with its colour nuances: the cool greys of marble or the soft, biscuity tones of stone. At night, full of blazing logs, it holds a room in thrall, creating an intimate and relaxed atmosphere. But no fireplace is perfect. This one is dark and imposing and tends to overwhelm the room. It needs a bold decorating hand to restore equilibrium to the sitting room.*

There is a subtle difference between balancing the weight of a dominant feature in the context of a room – which is a positive exercise – and trying to camouflage it. In this room, the fireplace is a glorious celebration of all things Victorian: heavy slate, marble panels and intricate, decorative tiles. The issue is not whether the fireplace looks good, but whether the black, salmon and parchment colour scheme are out of step in a family sitting room. For a space that needs to be vital and stimulating, working a scheme around its prevailing dark tones is not a sensible option.

The answer lies in a confident decorative approach. Bold, daring patterns and large, chunky furniture with a strong personality

will move attention away from the fireplace and around the room. A striking apple green, just glimpsed among the fireplace tiles, forms the seed of an idea for a vivacious, contemporary revamp.

**Above** A fireplace can be multi-faceted. Examine it for themes to be drawn out, specks of colour awaiting discovery, or textural hints within rough-hewn stone, or stately marble.

**Left and Opposite** The generous proportions of a wide bay window and the gift of day-long sunshine are not enough to counteract a heavy, dark fireplace. However, colour-drenched walls and the confident mixing of abstract patterns turn an unexceptional room into a comfortable, vibrant family sitting room.

**Right** Large-scale pattern repeats
call for careful planning. Start off
with a standard-sized colour board
and amass the different shades
and companion fabrics, then bring
home show-length pieces of material
to try out in the room itself.

**Above** Highlight a single motif
from an abstract or pictorial
pattern in a panel on a cushion.
A border in a toning or contrasting
textile, with or without piping, will
give the design a fresh slant.
Intersperse heavily patterned
cushions with simply tailored plain
cushions, featuring self-
buttoning, pintucks or ties.

## Shifting the focus

There are some large-scale, abstract motifs that cannot help
but distract and it is these that form the nucleus of the room's
new look. Large-scale patterns call for strong, vibrant walls to
maintain equilibrium. You may think that this room, with its
lofty ceiling and generous bay window, provides the perfect
space for experimenting with samples of wild, wacky wallpaper,
but this will only fight with the fireplace rather than playing
it down. Instead, apple green instantly tempers the dark hues
of the fireplace, and adds vibrancy and modernity to the room.

For the windows, a crisp cotton sporting a stylized daisy in
denim blue and honey hangs as curtains, a wide, navy border

**Opposite** Here picture and print
choices have been left until last.
Their variegated tones are used to
draw out particular shades in
the scheme. A plain linen mount
or handpainted frame could also be
chosen to echo a vivid accent shade.

around the leading edge drawing your attention. Roman blinds in a pencil-thin denim stripe add to the effect. In addition, a Madras check in denim blue and apple green covers the sofa which, placed opposite the fireplace, serves to balance it.

Once started, the mixture of patterns gathers momentum. The bolder the mix of designs, the more they seem to call for additional patterns to give them a third dimension. Tiny checks are natural mixers, as are stripes or abstract prints. However, any further pattern on the armchairs might be unsettling, so deeper blues, running to indigo and navy, define their shape as well as being more appropriate near to the dark hearth.

Where patterns compete, there should be unifying strands to join the elements together. In this room, the cushions create that unity. Each one is unique, yet each one is also a reflection of another textile in the room. A single daisy forms a central panel, the pencil stripe a broad border, apple-coloured linen and unbroken madras check are used for contrast piping. Using the remnants from curtains, blinds and covers is a foolproof way of anchoring an entire scheme and reiterating its themes.

Flooring should not be an afterthought in a busy scheme. It needs to be considered and matched with key textiles. A sitting room needs flooring that is comfortable and durable, yet smart and attractive. Where dark floorboards may have muddied the other colours, a tightly knit honey sisal gives a clean finish.

**Opposite** A stunning fireplace deserves to be dressed up. Draw attention to it with candles, scented or otherwise, for atmosphere, with piled-up logs and a fireside chair close by. Try to keep the traditional mantelpiece clutter of invitations, letters and keys at bay.

**Above** Weave grown-up detailing into a family-centred room. A gilded candelabra comes into its own by night.

**Right** Make accessories work. Matt cream and spun gold plant pots reflect the contrast of cream-painted wooden furniture and elaborate gilded detailing.

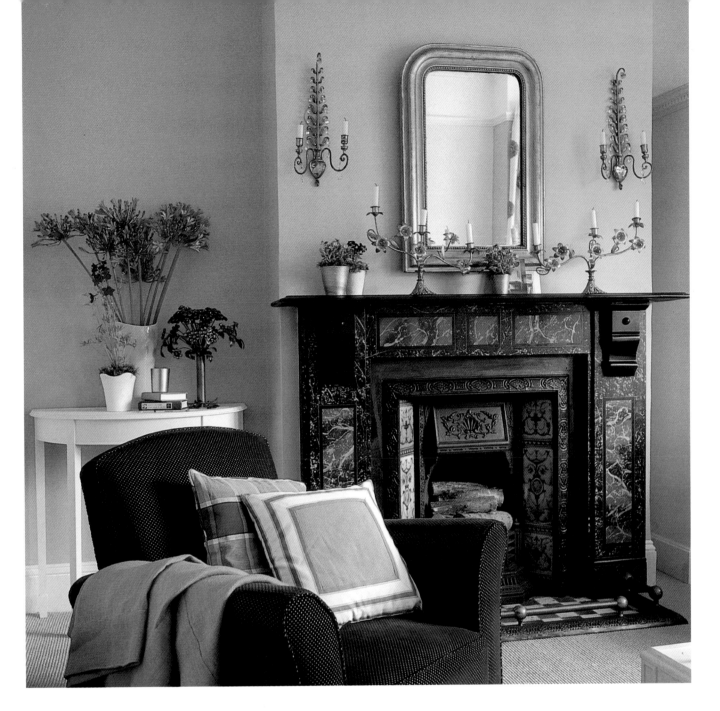

## Defining the fireplace

However beautiful its composition, or curvaceous its lines, a fireplace may need a little help to fulfil its potential. Pay attention to what it is doing in the room. If the fireplace is to be used at night for a spectacular real fire, the hearth can be piled high with logs, while coals are kept in a basket alongside gleaming fire tools and a guard. If the fireplace is a purely decorative feature, perhaps a delicate needlepoint firescreen is all that is needed to set it off. What goes above the fireplace, and what is arranged on the mantelpiece, is important, too.

The dense materials of this fireplace, heavy slate and marble, need to be offset by lighter touches. A mirror is essential for maximizing light and counteracting the dark mantelpiece, and its thick, golden frame works just as well with the clear, fresh green of the walls as with the dark tones below. Gilded and elaborately branched candelabra set with creamy candles are pretty by day and glint in the mirror at night, transforming a family room into an atmospheric drawing room. The wall-mounted candelabra add still more sparkle and shine.

# A Decorative Entrance

*A period house is crammed with patterns cut into glass, carved into wood or traced within ironwork. A hallway is as good a starting point as any. Look to the colours and designs of original floor tiles for inspiration, and upwards to a fanlight of wonderful coloured glass. The fretwork detailing of this hallway arch resembles a Caribbean beach house, prompting the choice of soft, ice-cream colours for an upbeat start.*

**Above** The intricate lines of a finely wrought motif or the twist of a rail may contain the kernel of a decorative idea.

**Right** From a standard, narrow high-traffic area to one with its own charm, this Edwardian hall gets a radical facelift.

**Opposite** The Caribbean flavour of the original archway inspires a dreamy eau-de-Nil and aqua scheme, which harmonizes with the encaustic tiled floor.

A hallway is the gateway to the rest of the house. It is where we say hello and goodbye, linger on the telephone, hurry up and down stairs, deposit bags and open mail. It is a high-traffic area, most likely to have its floors soiled with mud and its walls scraped with buggies. For all these reasons, it should be planned as a light and uplifting place, practical enough to withstand all this action while exuding a warm and welcoming ambience.

This hallway benefits from being sunny and wide. It has a pair of attractive double doors and the archway creates a natural visual pause before the corridor and stairs beyond. Dense, creamy colour forms part of the plan, but so too does the pursuit of that all-important atmosphere.

## Stamping a personality

However intricate its detailing, however sunny its aspect, a hallway is generally a cold and draughty place, with a hard floor underfoot and no furniture to lend it charm. It is for this reason that the spectrum of Caribbean shades – marshmallow pink, lemon yellow, leaf green, sea aqua and blue – is so tempting. Although they are all refreshing, light-refracting colours, the aqua shade works best here.

The colour scheme in a hallway is as important for the rooms leading off it as it is for the space itself. If you select a shade that is too definite, it will jar with the colour scheme of adjoining rooms. Aqua sits happily with white, neutrals and similarly toned colours, and it also fits in well with the chalky blue, sand and terracotta tiles underfoot. Suggestive of sunny skies and warmth, aqua captures the light and chases away the cold.

A hallway also needs furniture to give it personality, form and atmosphere. This is not an impossibility: the narrowest of corridor halls invariably has a radiator which can be transformed with a slim decorative cover. Wall-mounted hooks will suffice where a cupboard will not fit. This hallway is wide enough to take a tall, antique hall stand, which easily accommodates the mail, keys and bags below, and its quirky detailing adds character. A Swedish console, with fretwork around the sides, turns a corridor into a telephone area, and reiterates in a simpler form the fretwork of the decorative arch.

Textures do not often come to mind when you think of a typical hallway. Painted walls and flooring are usually the sum total. Yet the contrast of rough and smooth, shiny and matt, are powerful mood creators. Here, the smoothness of the original tiles is contrasted with the practical, tough weave of the jute herringbone carpet on the stairs; the bumpy detail of

embossed wallpaper is set against the pebble-smooth glass of a door handle traced in silver. It is rare to find textiles in a hall, but they are very good for softening empty spaces. Left unadorned, these glass doors might seem too open, admitting not only bright light, but cold draughts and prying eyes, too. Narrow roll-up blinds in silky seersucker with a satin trim prettify and filter the sunlight. Their surprise factor has as much impact as their soft and subtle texture.

## A repeated image

An architectural feature with a dominant motif – a leaf that can be copied, a swirl that can be reinterpreted – should be exploited to the full. The carefree loops and clover-leaf shapes found in the archway are drawn onto a radiator cover and cut out; this not only continues the pattern theme but provides essential ventilation too. The swooping tendrils from the archway are also echoed in the curly metal chandelier dangling by the porch.

**Above** Rooms are often decorated with flowers, and a hall space should be no exception. Consider both colour and scent. A bunch of flowers can create a welcoming, perfumed threshold.

**Opposite** Connecting spaces, like narrow halls and corridors, are frequently neglected in favour of the rooms that open from them. To reverse that trend, make use of flowers and pictures, or artfully arranged *objet d'art*, to create a tableau that can just be glimpsed from the front door – a promise of colour and style to come.

**Right** A radiator cover can be customized to capitalize on a distinctive motif or an architectural feature. Keep the look abstract, or copy it exactly, but do so with a spirit of improvization and a lightness of touch. These Edwardian swirls and clover leaves take on a contemporary look when transposed as cut-outs for a radiator cover.

# TRAVEL

Travel provokes a fresh perspective, bringing with it new inspiration and throwing the familiar elements of our life sharply into focus. Journeying abroad imprints fresh images on our minds —

exhilarating, jumbled, colourful — and enables us to bring new experiences to bear on our normal environment. Little wonder that designers travel the globe seeking new influences in far-flung places, distilling what they see into a new trend. Try to do the same. It might be visual memories that inspire, the dark, bitter colours and rough textures of tribal handicrafts seen in a market, a fleeting glimpse of hot sun on a colourwashed wall; or a treasured item, loved and brought home. Atmosphere plays a part, too: the serenity of a cool, painted church; the relaxing flutter of a curtain at a beach-house window.

## SOURCES OF INSPIRATION

Any one influence from abroad could be interpreted in a decorative scheme, but it is always necessary to learn to explore and anchor them in practical terms, adapting foreign styles to your own interior.

It is a rare traveller who returns home without a few treasures, and an even rarer one who does not throw most of them away. Mistakes happen because we do not focus sufficiently on what we might do with a tribal textile or handpainted pot once we are back home. Yet there are always beautiful, stimulating souvenirs that can not only be integrated into our houses, but also used as a source of inspiration. So, shop a little more judiciously, keeping in mind how your home looks. Textiles, such as Thai silks in myriad colours or striped Greek mattress ticking, are very likely to hold their appeal once home, and could play a major part in a scheme; whereas a handstitched Indian cushion cover is more likely destined to be an accessory. You may be inspired by a piece or style of furniture, perhaps a Peruvian carved bench, but think hard before you ship one home. It is amazing how seeing lots of a particular

thing while you are abroad makes you think you just cannot do without one. Far better to take a photograph, consider it, and if you still like it once you are home, look for something similar.

Every region and country has its own distinctive decorative style that will provoke new ideas. Whether you are actually travelling or simply looking through books on foreign interiors, analyse the details of the things that attract you. Is it the style of furniture, unusual paint colours and combinations, or the different textures common to other climates? When you have defined the appeal, you can then select appropriate details for your own scheme. Do not attempt to copy an entire look; go instead for your own unique interpretation of it. The natural light, architectural styles, and particular atmospheres born of cultural variations, simply will not translate verbatim to another country.

When you travel, attempt to assimilate the more abstract nuances of atmosphere, image, colour and light that surround you. You do not have to be in far-flung

**Opposite, above** Pale silvery tongue-and-groove panelling and rustic gingham-edged curtains have their origins in an Alpine retreat or lakeside log cabin. A simple stone sink, abstract pictures, the wood detailing and brick floor all help to make this a warmly welcoming bathroom.

**Right** The indigenous style of a piece of furniture – even a textile bedspread – may hint at a country visited and remembered. In this bedroom, the dark wooden chairs, the artfully arranged bamboo, and yellow Chinese panels in the bathroom screen discreetly suggest an Oriental mood.

**Opposite, below** Grand palaces and churches, ethnic houses and shrines, all steeped in their own culture and decorative style, are imprinted on our memory as we travel. This bedroom's faded tones evoke centuries-old plaster and give it a romantic mood that is further enhanced by well-chosen furniture. An eighteenth-century French *Bergère* bed, rumpled bedlinen and stone corbel bedside tables all help to conjure up European elegance at its finest.

**Left** This intriguing room takes elements from around the world. There are colonial chairs, an *ikat* cushion, kilim rugs, a tooled-leather box and tribal pots. The creative mix works because the deliberately neutral walls provide a blank canvas.

**Opposite** Sizzling and intense colours, seen abroad and adapted for use at home with appropriate textures, are lavishly cheerful and warm. A heady mix of tangerine walls and amethyst paintwork, tribal paintings and an explosion of rich textures and patterns, make this room lusciously welcoming and unforgettable.

places to glean valuable inspiration, but your responses may be fresher to unfamiliar and perhaps more dramatic regions. A turquoise sky hovering over the sandy wastes of African scrubland may inspire you to put together blues and browns you would never have considered before. The bright light on a February day in New York, combined with urban textures and the steely blue of the sky, might provoke a subtler scheme. As you travel, use your camera, your memory, a sketchbook, or a diary to capture these influences in much the same way as a writer or artist might keep notes for future works.

## TRAVEL INFLUENCES

Tapping into foreign influences and styles is a skill in itself. Adapting and anchoring some of them into your overall scheme is more complex. If the hues of a piece of fabric or a unique piece of furniture attract you, then follow the principles set out in earlier chapters for putting a scheme together. But analysing the appeal of texture, surface and colour variations to see what inspires us is vital; as is picking out cultural and native stylistic differences. Only when we can do this can we begin to copy or adapt the effects to recreate their mood, or define a new style.

When you travel you cannot fail to notice the effects of colour; its intensity in Mediterranean countries, or along a California coast, or the slightly chalkier pastels daubed throughout the Caribbean. They are seen inside and outside buildings, bursting forth from textiles, and painted on pots. They are there because they work with bright, hot sunshine, and are in tune with the surreal vividness of native fruits, flowers and vegetables. Which is why, if you live in colder climes, it is unwise to adopt them unmodified in your home, no matter how much you love them. In cool northern light, they lose much of their bite and appeal. Instead, pick one or two shades, lemon sherbet or Mediterranean blue, say, and reinterpret them in fabrics, perhaps strong cotton or linen, rather than as overpowering wall colours. Mix in neutrals as a link with your less-than-brilliant light and perhaps more sombre natural surroundings, and the adaptation will work.

Then there is texture. Buildings in hot countries are crammed with ceramic tiles, marble, mosaics and tinted plaster. For those of us in more northerly climates, the allure is their contrast to the materials used at home – wool carpet, tapestry, thick cotton, matt paint or paper on walls. They also appeal because they remind us of atmospheres, the sudden contrast between heat outside and the welcome coolness and smoothness of the textures within. However, skilful adaptation is important. If you cannot live without the brilliance of blue Moroccan mosaic tiles, do not use them on every surface; the final effect could be cold and clinical. Try them as detailing on a kitchen shelf or in patterns on a bathroom floor, and match their intense colour with others in softer textures – vivid red towels, perhaps, or a simple blind. Similarly, a southern traveller in northern climes may fall in love with a heavy pure wool carpet but would be unwise to use it at home for any-thing more than a bedside rug. Some surfaces, such as

the warm tones of Italian palazzo walls, do translate more readily to cooler countries and their architecture. However, think carefully about other styles to match with them. A casual mix of white linen covers or more formal ruched silk curtains may look good individually and feel more natural than using only authentic Italian furniture. A sudden passion for large-scale stone blocks may have been inspired by a visit to a European city palace. A paint-effect wallpaper will recreate such a look, but use it with a sense of humour, and paper somewhere unexpected, like a bathroom.

Window and fabric treatments are directly affected by the rise and fall of temperature which, of course, varies from one country to the next. Take stylistic details from the Greeks, who might hang an unlined fabric panel to float in whatever breeze there is at a window or door. Observe the way the French often opt for narrow dress curtains pulled aside with tiebacks to leave a plain blind screening the sun. Look at the motifs cut out of the thick wooden shutters on Austrian chalets or the gathered gingham pelmets (valances) teamed with thin voile curtains so beloved of the Swedes. Whether you are in a chic hotel or a stately home abroad, take note of any differences in the way that the beds are dressed, from canopies to sheets. Are cushion covers in unusual styles and shapes? Do they use conventional tablecloths or go for long, thin, runners? Observe, too, how patterns and textiles are used in foreign countries. Staying in a French château might just inspire you to try a classic combination of antique toile de Jouy with fresh checks. You might adopt a single batik print seen in Indonesia, reworked as cushions on a plain sofa at home.

Inevitably, there will be souvenirs – lamps, rugs, pictures, ceramics – that are not destined to be interpreted, but can be worked into your scheme to remind you of a happy trip. You can adapt these things, too. If a Madonna image from Spain looks overly gaudy in its gilded frame, reframe it in dark wood. Embroidered white sheets from Hong Kong would look cosier mixed with a rustic blanket. Those too-bright Indian saris you intended for curtains can be cut up and inserted as panels in plainer cushion covers. Edit and adapt, and do not be afraid to lose a 'find' that does not fit in.

## MODERN TRAVEL INFLUENCES

When we travel it is the rustic, cultural, and historical aspects of unfamiliar designs and colours that provide stimulating contrasts to what we know at home. Yet, travel is also an opportunity to look at the modern, minimalist interior decor that is favoured in the chic, design-conscious centres of the world – London, New York, Milan, Paris, Tokyo. Travelling out of familiar territory is often the only opportunity we get to see genuinely contemporary furniture or gadgets, and the *crème de la crème* of the latest designs. Immersing yourself in unfamiliar furniture with new shapes, wheels, unexpected colours and finishes, while in a foreign city, can be remarkably stimulating. You may come home with an uncharacteristic enthusiasm to try something contemporary, or, having experienced a minimalist Italian bathroom, you might want to jettison your roll-top bath in favour of something sleek, marble and understated.

## THE GRAND FINALE

Wanting to decorate with a difference and to go beyond the common melting pot of influences gives added impetus to travel. Most of us know the combination of hassle and satisfaction that you experience as you

haul a Turkish rug or stash of rustic china onto the plane, but
not everything is so easily transportable. Fortunately, many
companies import, adapt and market most of the inspirational
pieces that we see on our travels. You will almost certainly be
able to find hand-loomed Indian cottons, Thai and Indian silks,
Provençal tiles in myriad colours, Spanish terracotta slabs,
and African slate. You can buy chunky Greek day beds by
mail order, or Indian fretwork furniture and Indonesian painted
cupboards, traditional American milk paints, and Mediterranean
paint washes. Scour ethnic areas in town for Chinese textiles
and lacquered boxes, Indian fabrics, and African baskets. Track
down specialist suppliers of a particular style, such as Swedish
or American Shaker furniture, or maybe Portuguese needlepoint rugs. It is worth the search, because one special piece that
utterly captures the atmosphere of a far-away place can give
the most wonderful grand finale to your scheme.

**Opposite** When you are abroad, a pile
of cobalt-blue tiles, an Indian bench,
or hand-woven textiles, seen *in situ* or
for sale, may be irresistible. If so, how
you interpret and adapt them to your
own environment is vital. Perhaps use
tiles in smaller quantities, as
splashbacks or counter-tops; or limit
bright paint colours to the woodwork.
Before an imported element is
permanently installed at home, live
with it for a while to ensure that its
transition works and that your
enthusiasm for it has survived.

**Above** Travel provides a feast of
extraordinary sights. Interpreting the
spirit of a place and allowing its style
to influence your decorating may be
more interesting than trying
to reproduce it in total. In this
informal dining room, vivid hues from
Greece – hot pink, aqua, lilac and
orange – combine with tiny twinkling
lights, a mosaic mirror and casual
country furniture, for a quirky
effect that defies definition.

# A Memorable Journey

*A trip to foreign lands can prompt unique and surprising thoughts. A landscape glimpsed through a train window, the grainy light of a winter's day or the sun-drenched colour in an unfamiliar clime could all provide the stimulus for a new slant on a favourite room. Dignified and serene, this country dining room borrows casually from Sweden's cool Gustavian style. Faux-panelled walls and crisp stripes are played out in gentle tones of tea-rose, white and chalky grey.*

Gathering together the strands of a foreign style is all about interpretation, rather than recreation. Identify classic themes, a dominant mood, and characteristic motifs, shapes or hues. Then adapt them with a light touch to suit your particular room. The appeal of a Swedish look lies in the mix of the known and unknown, the familiar and the strange. Just one authentic feature – a piece of furniture or an original textile – may form the nucleus of the scheme to come. The investment here is in a good reproduction Swedish dining table and medallion chairs which set the right tone.

A dining room benefits from a poised and formal style which creates the perfect setting for intimate dinners. This low-ceilinged room is rural rather than ornate, and lacks the necessary sophistication to carry off grand furniture. To create a more graceful and elegant space, the walls are painted with *trompe-l'oeil* panels; these give a suggestion of faded grandeur and place the room in an historic context.

**Opposite** The original sage green walls and chintz curtains were oppressive in this small country room. Pale, airy colours and *trompe-l'oeil* panelling produce a fresher effect.

**Above** A breathtaking landscape may unleash a new vein of inspiration, as the glint of sun on snow provokes a move towards an unexplored palette.

**Left** Harking back to a forgotten era of elegance and grace, this peaceful dining room is resplendent with harmonious colours and lovely furniture. It represents the perfect fusion of the best of Gustavian style, with its simple stripes and ornate detailing, combined with a twist of English country prettiness.

**Left** Identifying a motif characteristic of a certain style is the starting point for soft furnishings. The classic Gustavian two-colour pencil stripe is teamed with ticking stripes in varying scales, and a simple Swedish floral. Mixing stripes is infinitely easier when sticking to a rigid colour framework. Strawberry, tea-rose, pearly greys and charcoal form this basic palette.

**Below** The way that the furniture is arranged in a room is as important as the shapes of the pieces them-selves. A single chair against a wall sums up the pared-down style integral to the Gustavian interior.

**Opposite** When choosing furniture, do not feel too constrained about finding faithful reproductions. Look instead for shapes that feel right and have a similar mood. The curvy cabriole legs, washed grey tones and simple loop handles of this antique commode mix sympathetically with the reproduction table and chairs. A spacious chest of drawers in a dining room is invaluable, too, for storing extra table linen, utensils and candles.

## Adapting a look

When travelling abroad, it is often the unfamiliar slant of light that lends a magical air to an otherwise ordinary interior. In hot countries, it is the contrast of light and shade that is novel and exciting, the brilliance of colour followed by the bleaching of the sun. More northerly climes shimmer subtly in cool, grey light. So recreating the shifting nuances of Sweden's soft, diffuse light is a natural starting point for the dining room. A combination of restful greys, from charcoal to chalk, will achieve this and will work with rather than against the lack of light in the room. Pale grey paint for the walls, a tone lighter on the ceiling, and a shade darker on the paintwork; two hand-mixed greys outline the faux panels, one with a blue bias and one tending towards brown.

Inspiration for painted faux panels can be found in a quick glance through coffee-table books devoted to Swedish style. Even the grandest Swedish palace used simple paint effects to suggest panelling, and it is a technique that is much easier than it looks. Masking tape provides the only guide you need for keeping the lines straight.

The tonal build-up of greys means that a secondary shade is needed to soften and define the dining room. Faded, soft reds running to pink are classically Swedish. So, too, are striped textiles which are the staples of the Gustavian look. A pink narrow variety covers the dining chairs, plus a broader stripe to fill the deep window seat, and a bolder cherry-red stripe for a scatter cushion. To break up what could easily become an over-abundance of stripes, a delicately drawn Swedish cotton floral is introduced into the scheme.

If you are attempting to reinvent a particular look, you will need to go further than a simple selection of fabrics; it is the way you employ them that is important. Swedish loose-cover styles are characteristically relaxed and simply tailored, so tie-on seat covers for the medallion dining chairs are just right. Where an English armchair might sport a box-pleated skirt, here the covers are simple and slightly baggy with the chair legs on full show. You can learn a great deal about loose furniture coverings simply by scrutinizing books on foreign style, or by visiting museums and grand houses. Be prepared to adapt certain elements. Where a Swedish pelmet (valance) may be an understated frill of muslin, a more substantial choice is essential here. Two embroidered antique sheets are hung together for curtains and the top is flipped over to create a ruffled effect.

**Above** A dining room provides myriad opportunities for expanding on pretty motifs and adding new strands. Think of pictorial china for the table, self-patterned linens, etched glasses and wonderful cutlery (flatware). Here handblown rustic wine glasses work well with exotically patterned French porcelain because they reflect the mix of styles already forged in the room.

**Opposite, below** In a pale, colour-washed scheme, where pearly greys predominate and the play of light is essential to the look, gentle rather than vivid accent shades are needed. Consider using glass to achieve unusual effects. Tinted wine glasses, glowing against white table linen, are one option here, but so too are glass vases, bowls or a chandelier tinged with glints of extra colour.

**Right** Adaptation is always essential when reinterpreting a look seen abroad. The ways in which a sofa is covered and the manner in which a window is dressed contain vital clues. If a loose cover is a simple, stitched linen slip, then keep your cushions in a similar vein: buttoned, self-panelled or totally unadorned.

## Essential embellishments

When dipping into an unfamiliar style, there are fewer restrictions on what you can and cannot do. In the end, the choices are essentially about what pleases you and what is right for the room. Yet an analysis of a particular style should still be thorough, so you really do achieve the best effect. The enduring appeal of a Swedish Gustavian style is its air of elegance tinged with simplicity, so the finishing touches need to reflect this mix. A romantic glass chandelier, a heavily ornate mirror and side table, and ceramics painted with cherries and curlicues all provide the necessary elegance, while plain silver candlesticks, heavy linen napkins and an unframed oil painting represent the element of restraint. A cluster of strawberry-pink country roses, gathered into an unpretentious glass vase, reflects on a small scale what the entire room achieves.

# STOCKISTS

## PAINTS

**Papers and Paints**
4 Park Walk
London SW10 0AD
(Vast range of colours, including historical shades.)

**Farrow & Ball**
249 Fulham Road
London SW3 6HY
(Muted, historical shades including the National Trust range of paints.)

**Fired Earth**
Twyford Mill
Oxford Road, Adderbury
Oxon OX17 3HP
(Range of V& A historical paint colours.)

**Sanderson**
112–120 Brompton Road
London SW3 1JJ
(Spectrum range of 1,350 colours.)

**Dulux Advice Centre**
ICI Paints
Wexham Road, Slough
Berkshire SL2 5DS
(Over 1,600 colours, plus Heritage historical colours.)

**Paint Library**
5 Elystan Street
London SW3 3NT
(Classic and contemporary colours.)

**Brats**
281 King's Road
London SW3 5EW
(Water-based Mediterranean paints.)

**Francesca's Lime Wash**
Unit 24a, Battersea Business Centre
99–109 Lavender Hill
London SW11 5QL
(Traditional, textured paint finishes in warm, soft colours.)

## WALLPAPERS

**Ornamenta**
3–12 Chelsea Harbour
  Design Centre
London SW10 0XE
(Collection includes faux stone, cloudscape and woodgrain designs.)

**Cole & Son**
144 Offord Road
London N1 1NS
(Mainly archive wallpapers, including grand designs.)

## FABRIC & WALLPAPER CO-ORDINATES

**Cath Kidston**
8 Clarendon Cross
London W11 4AP
(Pretty retro florals.)

**Designers Guild**
275–277 King's Road
London SW3 5EN
(Vivid, painterly prints, plus checks, plains, voiles.)

**Jane Churchill**
151 Sloane Street
London SW1X 9BX
(Fresh, contemporary checks, florals, voiles, weaves.)

**Colefax & Fowler**
110 Fulham Road
London SW3 6RL
(Classic chintzes, plus extensive weaves.)

**Liberty Furnishings**
304 King's Road
London SW3 5UH
(Bold and smaller scale florals, on cotton and voile.)

**Osborne & Little**
304 King's Road
London SW3 5UH
(Diverse range including prints and weaves.)

## FABRICS

**Ian Mankin**
109 Regent's Park Road
London NW1 8UR
(Excellent selection of cottons, linens, ginghams, tickings.)

**Moygashel**
Moygashel Mills
Moygashel
County Tyrone
Northern Ireland BT71 7QS
(Pure linens in every colour.)

**The Natural Fabric Company**
Wessex Place
127 High Street
Hungerford
Berkshire RG17 0DL
(Good range of tickings, ginghams, hessians, denims and tartans.)

**Henry Bertrand**
11 Melton Street
London NW1 2EA
(Fantastic choice of silks in every colour and weight.)

**Ciel Decor**
187 New King's Road
London SW6 4SW
(Traditional Provençal fabrics, also distributors for Souleiado and Les Olivades.)

**The Malabar Cotton Company**
31-33 The South Bank
  Business Centre
Ponton Road
London SW8 5BL
(Indian cottons and silks, from plains to huge checks.)

**Pierre Frey**
251–253 Fulham Road
London SW3 6HY
(French fabrics, including toiles.)

## FURNITURE

**Habitat**
196 Tottenham Court Road
London W1P 9LD
(Contemporary, well-priced furniture.)

**The Conran Shop**
81 Fulham Road
London SW3 6RD
(Modern and classic furniture.)

**IKEA**
255 North Circular Road
London NW10 0JQ
(Modern, clean designs at reasonable prices.)

**Heal's**
196 Tottenham Court Road
London W1P 9LD
(Contemporary, classic furniture.)

**Judy Greenwood Antiques**
657 Fulham Road
London SW6 5PY
(Period French pieces.)

**Decorative Living**
55 New King's Road
London SW6 4SE
(Unusual decorative antiques.)

**The Iron Bed Company**
Terminus Road
Chichester
West Sussex PO19 2ZZ
(New iron bedsteads in classic and contemporary styles.)

**Grand Illusions**
2–4 Crown Road
Twickenham TW1 3EE
(Painted or waxed pieces, from
armoires to dressers.)

**Hart Villa**
6 Mount Farm
Churchill, Nr Chipping Norton
Oxfordshire OX7 6NP
(Traditional upholstery styles.)

**Scumble Goosie**
Lewiston Mill
Toadsmore Road
Brimscombe, Stroud
Gloucestershire GL5 2TB
(Ready to paint furniture
including Gustavian tables and
French armoires.)

**The Blue Door**
74 Church Road
London SW13 0DQ
(Gustavian copies, plus Swedish
antiques.)

**Sasha Waddell at Codrington
Furniture**
Arch 80, Chelsea Bridge Business
 Centre
Queenstown Road
London SW8 4NE
(Swedish inspired furniture.)

## FLOORING
**The Alternative Flooring
Company**
14 Anton Trading Estate, Andover
Hampshire SP10 2NJ
(Natural flooring including coir,
sisal, seagrass, jute, all wool.)

**Natural Flooring Direct**
Freepost Lon 1229
London SE16 4BR
(Mail order only sisal, coir, jute,
seagrass and wool mixes.)

**Roger Oates Design**
The Long Barn, Eastnor, Ledbury
Herefordshire HR8 1EL
(Traditional striped stair runners
in natural fibres.)

**Sinclair Till**
791–793 Wandsworth Road
London SW8 3JQ
(Wide choice of linos; patterns
customized to order)

**Wicanders**
Amorim, Amorim House
Star Road, Partridge Green
Horsham, West Sussex RH13 8RA
(Wooden and cork flooring.)

**Junckers**
Wheaton Court Centre
Wheaton Road, Witham
Essex CM8 3UJ
(Wide range of solid hardwood
floors.)

## NEW ZEALAND
**Abacus Flooring Services**
375 Dominion Road
Mt. Eden
Auckland

**Context Wallcoverings**
The Axis Building
1 Cleveland Road
Parnell
Auckland

**Cucire Designer Fabrics Ltd.**
Shop 11, Harbour City Centre
Wellington

**The Fabric Warehouse**
25 Hutt Road
Wellington

**Levenes**
Pacific Plaza
Whangaparoa

**Luraflex Window Fashions**
22 Burmingham Drive
Riccarton
Christchurch

**Uniflex Furnishings Ltd.**
29 Keeling Road
Henderson
Auckland

**The Wooded Floor Co. Ltd.**
74–78 Sale Street
Auckland Centre
Auckland

## AUSTRALIA
**Academy Tiles**
20 Herbert Street
Artamon
NSW 2064

**Architectural & Design Centre**
664 Botany Road
Alexandria
NSW 2015

**Dulux Australia**
McNaughton Road
Clayton
Victoria 3168

**Home Hardware**
414 Lower Dandenong Road
Braeside
Victoria 3195

**McEwans**
387–403 Bourke Street
Melbourne
Victoria 3000

**Romano Tiles**
126 Canterbury Road
Kilsyth
Victoria 3137

## SOUTH AFRICA
**The Furniture Guild**
325 Innes Road
Morningside
Durban

**Home Hardware**
Dick Kemp Street
Meadowdale
Johannesburg (Edenvale)

**Parker Floors**
P.O. Box 1071
Jukskei Park

**Sevens Decorating Warehouse**
242 D.F Malan Drive
Northcliff
Johannesburg

**Tile City**
31–33 Sivewright Avenue
New Doornfentein
Johannesburg

**Universal Paints**
Randburg
24 Hendrick Verwoerd Drive
Cnr. Dalmeny Road
Linden

**Vita Upholstery**
2nd Floor
204 Anderson Street
Johannesburg

## JAPAN
**Loving Design Centre**
Shinjuku Park Tower
3–7–1, Nishi-Shinjuku
Shinjuku-ku
Tokyo 163–10

# INDEX

# ACKNOWLEDGMENTS

## AUTHOR ACKNOWLEDGMENTS

*I dedicate this book to my husband Anthony, and my children Cicely and baby Felix, whose birth punctuated the writing of this book. With thanks to Denny Hemming, Catriona Woodburn, Rachel Davies and Alison Fenton at Conran Octopus, for their enthusiasm and tireless hard work on the book. Special thanks too, to the Homes & Gardens decorating teams, past and present, for their creative and inspirational transformations.*

## PICTURE ACKNOWLEDGMENTS

*We would like to thank the following photographers and organizations for their kind permission to reproduce the photographs in this book.*

1 Sandra Lane/Homes & Gardens/Robert Harding Syndication; 2–3 Polly Wreford/Homes & Gardens/Robert Harding Syndication; 4–5 Debi Treloar/ Homes & Gardens/Robert Harding Syndication; 6 Ben Edwards/Impact; 7 vt wonen; 8 above Jan Baldwin (Cathy O'Clery); 8 below Tony Jones/Robert Harding Picture Library; 9 above Jaques Dirand/The Interior Archive; 9 below Robert Frerck/Robert Harding Picture Library; 10–11 Polly Wreford/ Homes & Gardens/Robert Harding Syndication; 12–13 Marie-Pierre Morel (Postic, Reyre)/Marie Claire Maison; 13 John Miller/Robert Harding Picture Library; 14 Dennis Brandsma/vt wonen; 15 Pascale Chevallier (Michel Klein)/Agence Top; 16 above Trevor Richards/Homes & Gardens/Robert Harding Syndication; 16 below Christian Sarramon; 17 vt wonen; 18 Chris Chen/Belle Magazine; 19 Frank Brandwijk/vt wonen; 20 Andrew Wood /The Interior Archive (Charles Worthington); 21 Tim Beddow/The Interior Archive; 22 above Habitat UK; 22 below Andrew Wood/The Interior Archive; 23 David Churchill/ Arcaid(Stickland Coombe Architects); 24–29 Tom Leighton/Homes & Gardens/Robert Harding Syndication; 30–35 Debi Treloar/Homes & Gardens/ Robert Harding Syndication; 36–37 Jan Baldwin (Cathy O'Clery); 37 Adam Woolfitt/Robert Harding Picture Library; 38 Simon Brown/The Interior Archive; 39 above David Phelps; 39 below Richard Holt/Homes & Gardens/ Robert Harding Syndication; 40 James Merrell/Homes & Gardens/Robert Harding Syndication; 41 Solvi Dos Santos; 42 Rodney Weidland/Vogue Living; 43 left Henry Wilson/The Interior Archive; 43 right Hotze Eisma; 44 vt wonen; 45 Ray Main; 46–51 Pia Tryde/Homes & Gardens/Robert Harding Syndication; 52–55 Polly Wreford/Homes & Gardens/Robert Harding Syndication; 56–59 Debi Treloar/Homes & Gardens/Robert Harding Syndication; 60–61 Polly Wreford/Homes & Gardens/Robert Harding Syndication; 61 right Simon Kenny/Vogue Living; 62 Hotze Eisma; 63 Marie-Pierre Morel (Paula Navone, D. Rosensztroch); 64 Marie-Pierre Morel (D. Rosensztroch)/Marie Claire Maison; 65 vt wonen; 66 Solvi Dos Santos; 67 Tim Goffe/The Interior Archive; 68 Andreas von Einsiedel/ Homes & Gardens/Robert Harding Syndication; 69 Hotze Eisma; 70–75 Debi Treloar/ Homes & Gardens/Robert Harding Syndication; 76–77 Ray Main (Gottelier Home; Designers of Artwork Knitwear); 77 Patricia Aithie/Ffotograff; 78–79 Tim Beddow/The Interior Archive; 78 Solvi Dos Santos; 80 left Simon Upton/ The Interior Archive; 81 David Parmiter/ Homes & Gardens/Robert Harding Syndication; 82 Marie-Pierre Morel (Sty. C. Ardouin)/Marie Claire Maison; 83 Jan Baldwin (Cathy O'Clery); 84–89 Debi Treloar/Homes & Gardens/Robert Harding Syndication; 90–93 Debbie Patterson/Homes & Gardens/Robert Harding Syndication; 94 Simon Upton/ World of Interiors; 95 Simon Brown/The Interior Archive; 96–97 Paul Ryan/International Interiors (Designer: Laura Bohn); 97 Fritz von der Schulenburg/ The Interior Archive; 98 Andrew Wood/The Interior Archive (Charles Worthington); 99 Nicolas Tosi (C. Ardouin)/Marie Claire Maison; 100 Christian Sarramon; 101 Otto Polman/Ariadne; 102–107 Polly Wreford/ Homes & Gardens/Robert Harding Syndication; 108 Simon Brown/The Interior Archive; 109 Jason Hawkes Aerial Collection/Julian Cotton Photo library; 110 Ray Main; 111 Hotze Eisma; 112 Andrew Wood/The Interior Archive; 113 Gilles de Chabaneix (sty. Marie Kalt)/Marie Claire Maison; 114 Marie-Pierre Morel (D. Rozenzstroch); 115 above Jan Verlinde (Pieter Vandenhout); 115 below Alexander van Berge; 116–121 Polly Wreford/Homes & Gardens/Robert Harding Syndication; 122 vt wonen; 123 Pascale Chevalier/ Agence Top(Nicole & Pierre de Fayet); 124 Andrew Wood/The Interior Archive; 125 Mads Mogensen; 126 Fritz von der Schulenburg/The Interior Archive; 127 vt wonen; 128 Simon Brown/The Interior Archive; 129 above Marie-Pierre Morel (Postic/ Reyre)/ Marie Claire Maison; 129 below Ariadne; 130–135 Debi Treloar/Homes & Gardens/Robert Harding Syndication; 136–141 Tom Leighton/Homes & Gardens/Robert Harding Syndication; 142 Marie-Pierre Morel (Sty: Christine Peuch)/Marie Claire Maison; 143 The Image Bank; 144 above Marie-Pierre Morel(Stylist: C. Ardouin)Marie Claire Maison; 144 below Lucinda Symons; 145 Simon Upton/ World of Interiors; 146 William Waldron (Sherrie Donghia); 147 Ray Main; 148–149 Henry Wilson/The Interior Archive; 150–155 Debi Treloar/Homes & Gardens/Robert Harding Syndication.